General Conference Addresses

JOURNAL EDITION | OCTOBER 2024

General Conference Addresses

JOURNAL EDITION | OCTOBER 2024

DESERET
BOOK

SALT LAKE CITY, UTAH

CONTENTS

SATURDAY EVENING SESSION

SUNDAY MORNING SESSION

SUNDAY AFTERNOON SESSION

Saturday Morning Session

OCTOBER 5, 2024

THE TRIUMPH OF HOPE

ELDER NEIL L. ANDERSEN

Of the Quorum of the Twelve Apostles

My dear brothers and sisters across the world, as we begin this very special time of general conference, the eyes of heaven will certainly be focused upon us. We will hear the voice of the Lord through His servants; we will feel the "guiding, directing, [and] comforting"[1] influence of the Holy Ghost, and our faith will be strengthened.

Three years ago, President Russell M. Nelson began general conference with these words: "Pure revelation for the questions in your heart will make this conference rewarding and unforgettable. If you have not yet sought for the ministering of the Holy Ghost to help you hear what the Lord would have you hear during these two days, I invite you to do so now. Please make this conference a time of feasting on messages from the Lord through His servants."[2]

The scriptures link three words powerfully together: faith, hope, charity. The gift of hope is a priceless endowment from God.[3]

The word *hope* is used for many things we want to happen. For example, "I hope it won't rain," or "I hope our team wins." My intent is to speak of our sacred and eternal hopes centered in Jesus Christ and the restored gospel and our "confident expectation[s] of . . . the promised blessings of righteousness."[4]

Our Hope for Eternal Life

Our hope of eternal life is assured through the grace of Christ and our own choices, allowing us the remarkable blessing of returning to our heavenly home and living forever in peace and happiness with our Heavenly Father, His Beloved Son, our faithful family and precious friends, and the righteous men and women from every continent and every century.[5]

On earth we experience joy and sorrow as we are tested and proven. Our victory comes through faith in Jesus Christ as we triumph over our sins, difficulties, temptations, unfairness, and the challenges of this mortal life.[6]

As we strengthen our faith in Jesus Christ, we see beyond our struggles to the blessings and promises of eternity. Like a light whose brilliance grows, hope brightens the darkened world, and we see our glorious future.

Hope Comes from God

Since the beginning, our Heavenly Father and His Beloved Son have eagerly blessed the righteous with the precious gift of hope.[7]

After leaving the garden, Adam and Eve were taught by an angel of the promise of Jesus Christ.[8] The gift of hope enlightened their lives. Adam declared, "My eyes are opened, and in this life I shall have joy."[9] Eve spoke of "the joy of [their] redemption, and the eternal life which God giveth unto all the obedient."[10]

Just as the Holy Ghost brought hope to Adam,[11] the power of the Lord's Spirit enlightens the faithful today, illuminating the reality of eternal life.

The Savior sends us a Comforter, the Holy Ghost, a companion bringing faith, hope, and peace "not as the world giveth."[12]

"In the world," the Savior said, "ye shall have tribulation: but be of good cheer [keep a brightness of hope]; I have overcome the world."[13]

In times of difficulty, we choose to trust the Lord in faith. We quietly pray, "Not my will but thine be done."[14] We feel the Lord's approval for our meek willingness, and we await the promised peace the Lord will send in His chosen timing.

The Apostle Paul taught, "The God of hope [will] fill you with . . . joy and peace . . . , that ye may abound in hope,"[15] "rejoicing in hope; patient in tribulation;"[16] "through the power of the Holy Ghost."[17]

A Lesson of Hope

The prophet Moroni knew firsthand about having hope in Christ during tribulation. He explained his harrowing situation:

"I am alone. . . . I have not . . . whither to go."[18]

"I make not myself known . . . lest they should destroy me."[19]

Remarkably, in this dark and lonely hour, Moroni records his father's words of hope:

3

"If a man have faith he must needs have hope; for without faith there cannot be any hope."[20]

"What is it that ye shall hope for? . . . Ye shall have hope through the atonement of Christ and the power of his resurrection, to be raised unto life eternal."[21]

My brothers and sisters, hope is a living gift, a gift that grows as we increase our faith in Jesus Christ. "Faith is the substance of things hoped for."[22] We build this substance—the evidence blocks of our faith—through prayer, temple covenants, keeping the commandments, continually feasting on the scriptures and the words of modern-day prophets, taking the sacrament, serving others, and worshipping weekly with our fellow Saints.

A House of Hope

To fortify our hope in a time of increasing wickedness, the Lord has directed His prophet to dot the earth with His temples.

As we enter the Lord's house, we feel the Spirit of God, verifying our hope.

The temple testifies of the empty tomb and that life beyond the veil continues for all.

For those who do not have an eternal companion, the ordinances powerfully confirm that every righteous person will receive every promised blessing.

There is sublime hope as a young couple kneels across the altar to be sealed, not just for time but for eternity.

There is an immensity of hope for us in the promises made to our posterity, whatever their current circumstances.

There is no pain, no sickness, no injustice, no suffering, nothing that can darken our hope as we believe and hold tightly to our covenants with God in the house of the Lord. It is a house of light, a house of hope.

When Hope Is Discarded

We shed tears of sorrow as we see the sadness and despair in those who have no hope in Christ.

I recently observed from a distance a couple who at one time had faith in Christ but then decided to discard their belief. They were successful in the world, and they found pleasure in their intellect and the rejection of their faith.

All seemed well until the husband, still young and energetic, suddenly fell ill and died. Like an eclipse of the sun, they had blocked the light of *the* Son, and the result was an eclipse of hope. The wife, in her disbelief, now felt disoriented, painfully unprepared, unable to comfort her children. Her intellect had told her that her life was in perfect order until suddenly she could see no tomorrow. Her despair brought darkness and confusion.

Hope in Heartbreaking Tragedy

Let me contrast her painful despair with another family's hope in Christ during a heartbreaking time.

Twenty-one years ago the newborn son of my nephew Ben Andersen and his wife, Robbie, was life-flighted from their Idaho farming community to Salt Lake City. I arrived at the hospital, and Ben explained the severe, life-threatening complications with their baby's heart. We placed our hands on Trey's tiny head. The Lord blessed him with continued life.

Trey had heart surgery the first week of his life, and more surgeries followed. As the years passed, it became apparent that Trey would need a heart transplant. Although his physical activities were limited, his faith expanded. He wrote, "I have never felt sorry for myself because I have always known the importance of having faith in Jesus Christ and a testimony of the plan of salvation."

Trey kept on his phone this well-known quote from President Nelson: "The joy we feel has little to do with the circumstances of our lives and everything to do with the focus of our lives."[23]

Trey wrote: "I have always looked forward to serving a full-time mission, but . . . my doctors won't let me serve a mission until at least a year after my transplant. . . . I've put my faith in Jesus Christ."

Trey was excited at being accepted into the accounting major at BYU beginning this semester, but even more excited in late July when he received the very anticipated telephone call to come to the hospital for his heart transplant.

"One year," Trey said, "and I will be on my mission."

There were great expectations as he entered the operating room. However, during the surgery there were devastating complications, and Trey never regained consciousness.

His mother, Robbie, said: "Friday had been the most heartbreaking day . . . just trying to wrap our minds around it. . . . I had stayed up late just trying to process everything. . . . But Saturday, I woke up with a feeling of absolute joy. It wasn't just peace; it wasn't denial. I felt joy for my son, and I felt joy as his mother. . . . Ben had gotten up a lot earlier than me, and when we finally got a chance to talk, Ben had awakened with the exact same feeling."[24]

Ben explained: "Clarity came to my soul as God taught me through His Holy Spirit. I awoke at 4:00 a.m. and was filled with indescribable peace and joy. How is this possible? . . . The passing of Trey is so very painful, and I miss him so much. But the Lord does not leave us comfortless. . . . I look forward to a joyful reunion."[25]

The Promise of Hope

Trey had noted in his journal these words from President Nelson's general conference talk: "It doesn't seem possible to feel joy when your child suffers with an incurable illness or when you lose your job or when your spouse betrays you. Yet that is precisely the joy the Savior offers. His joy is constant, assuring us that our 'afflictions shall be but a small moment' [Doctrine and Covenants 121:7] and be consecrated to our gain."[26]

Brothers and sisters, the peace you seek may not come as quickly as you desire, but I promise you that as you trust in the Lord, His peace will come.

May we nurture our precious faith, pressing forward with a perfect brightness of hope.[27] I testify that our hope is our Savior, Jesus Christ. Through Him, all our righteous dreams will be realized. He is the God of hope—the triumph of hope. He lives and He loves you. In the name of Jesus Christ, amen.

Notes

1. Russell N. Nelson, "Revelation for the Church, Revelation for Our Lives," *Ensign* or *Liahona*, May 2018, 96.
2. Russell M. Nelson, "Pure Truth, Pure Doctrine, and Pure Revelation," *Liahona*, Nov. 2021, 6–7.
3. "Have you noticed in the scriptures that hope seldom stands alone? Hope is often linked with faith. Hope and faith are commonly connected to charity. Why? Because hope is essential to faith; faith is essential to hope; faith and hope are essential to charity (see 1 Corinthians 13:13, Alma 7:24, Ether 12:28, Doctrine and Covenants 4:5). They support one another like legs on a three-legged stool. All three relate to our Redeemer.

    "*Faith* [is rooted in] Jesus Christ. *Hope* centers in his atonement. *Charity* is manifest in the 'pure love of Christ' (see Moroni 7:47). These three attributes are intertwined like strands in a cable and may not always be precisely distinguished. Together, they become our tether to the celestial kingdom" (Russell M. Nelson, "A More Excellent Hope" [Brigham Young University devotional, Jan. 8, 1995], 3, speeches.byu.edu).
4. Gospel Topics, "Hope," Gospel Library.
5. "Wherefore, whoso believeth in God might with surety hope for a better world, . . . even a place at the right hand of God, which hope cometh of faith, maketh an anchor to the souls of men, [making] them sure and steadfast" (Ether 12:4).
6. Elder Dieter F. Uchtdorf said: "Allow me to acknowledge that depression and other difficult mental and emotional challenges are real, and the answer is not simply, 'Try to be happier.' My purpose today is not to diminish or trivialize mental health issues. If you face such challenges, I mourn with you, and I stand beside you. For some people, finding joy may include seeking help from trained mental health professionals who devote their lives to practicing their very important art. We should be thankful for such help" ("A Higher Joy," *Liahona*, May 2024, 66).
7. Our Heavenly Father has declared that His work and glory is to bring to pass our eternal life (see Moses 1:39).
8. See Moses 5.
9. Moses 5:10.
10. Moses 5:11.
11. See Moses 5:9.
12. John 14:27.
13. John 16:33.
14. See Luke 22:42.
15. Romans 15:13.
16. Romans 12:12.
17. Romans 15:13.
18. Mormon 8:5.
19. Moroni 1:1.
20. Moroni 7:42.
21. Moroni 7:41.
22. Hebrews 11:1. In the Joseph Smith Translation it reads, "Faith is the *assurance* of things hoped for, the evidence of things not seen" (in the Bible appendix). We see the assurance of our faith in the blessings that come to those who keep the covenants they have made with the Lord.
23. Russell M. Nelson, "Joy and Spiritual Survival," *Ensign* or *Liahona*, Nov. 2016, 82.
24. Talk given by Robbie Andersen at the funeral of her son Trey Andersen, August 12, 2024. Trey had his surgery on July 31, 2024. He passed from this life on August 3, 2024.
25. Talk given by Ben Andersen at the funeral of his son Trey Andersen, August 12, 2024.
26. Russell M. Nelson, "Joy and Spiritual Survival," 82.
27. See 2 Nephi 31:20. The hope Nephi speaks of is perfect and bright because it is centered in Christ. He is perfect, and His Atonement, which offers this bright hope, is also perfect.

LIVE UP TO YOUR PRIVILEGES

PRESIDENT EMILY BELLE FREEMAN
Young Women General President

Recently my husband, Greg, received a diagnosis that would require an intensive surgery and months of chemotherapy. Like many of you who have faced a similar situation, we immediately began praying for heaven's help and God's power. The Sunday following Greg's surgery, the sacrament was delivered to our hospital room.

On this occasion, I was the only one taking the sacrament. One piece of bread. One cup of water. At church, my mind often focuses on the delivery system of the sacrament—the preparing, the blessing, and the passing. But on that afternoon, I pondered the gift of God's power available to me through the sacred ordinance itself and the covenant promise I was making as I took that piece of bread and that cup of water.[1] This was a time when I needed power from heaven. In the midst of great heartache, exhaustion, and uncertainty, I wondered about this gift that would allow me to draw upon the power from Him that I so desperately needed. Partaking of the sacrament would increase my companionship with the Spirit of the Lord,[2] allowing me to draw upon the gift of God's power, including the ministering of angels[3] and the Savior's enabling strength to overcome.

I don't think I had ever realized with this much clarity before that it's not only who officiates in the ordinance that matters—what the ordinance and our covenant promise unlock also deserves the focus of our attention.[4] Priesthood ordinances and covenant promises allow God to sanctify us and then work wonders in our lives. But how does this happen?[5]

First, in order for an ordinance to manifest the power of God in our lives, it must be done with authority from the Son of God. The delivery system is important. The Father entrusted Jesus Christ with the keys and authority to oversee the delivery of His priesthood ordinances. Under His direction, within the order of His priesthood, the sons of God have been ordained to stand *in place of* the Son of God.[6]

Second, we don't just make covenant promises—we must keep them. In many gospel ordinances, we make sacred covenants with

God; He promises to bless us as we *keep* those covenants.[7] Do we realize it is the combination of priesthood ordinances along with the keeping of covenant promises that allows us to draw upon God's power?

That afternoon I wondered if I, a covenant daughter of God, fully understood how to access the gift of God's power through priesthood ordinances and if I truly recognized how God's power works within me.[8]

In 2019 a prophetic invitation was extended to the women of the Church, teaching us how to draw the Savior's power into our lives. President Russell M. Nelson invited us to study Doctrine and Covenants 25, a revelation given to Emma Smith in Harmony, Pennsylvania.[9] Accepting that invitation changed my life.

Last month I had an unexpected opportunity to visit Harmony. There, under the maple trees, the priesthood was restored to Joseph Smith and Oliver Cowdery. Close to those trees is the front door of Joseph and Emma's home.[10] Across from the fireplace in that home there is a window. I stood at that window and wondered what Emma might have thought as she looked out across the trees.

In July of 1830, Emma was 26 years old; *she was so young.* She was three and a half years into her marriage. She had lost a baby boy—her first. His little grave is just down the lane from her home. As I stood at that window, it was not hard for me to imagine what might have filled her thoughts. Surely she worried about their finances, about the increasing persecution that threatened their safety, about their future. And yet the work of God was everywhere around her. Did she also wonder about her place in the plan, her purpose in His kingdom, and her potential in the eyes of God?

I think she may have.

Just across the way, the gift of God's priesthood authority and keys[11] had been restored to the earth.[12] This was a time when Emma actually needed power from heaven. In the midst of great heartache, exhaustion, and uncertainty, I imagine Emma wondered about this gift of God's priesthood that could unlock the power from Him that she so desperately needed.

But Emma didn't just stand at that window and wonder.

While the Prophet Joseph was being tutored in keys, offices, ordinances, and how to assist in the service of the priesthood, the Lord Himself, through His prophet, gave a revelation to Emma.[13] Not Nauvoo-Relief-Society-president Emma—this revelation was given to 26-year-old Emma in Harmony. Through revelation, Emma would learn about the inward sanctification and covenant connection that would increase the ability of those priesthood ordinances to work in her life.

First, the Lord reminded Emma of her place in His plan, including who she was and whose she was—a daughter in His kingdom.[14] She was invited to "walk in the paths of virtue,"[15] a path that included ordinances that would unlock God's power if Emma held on to her covenants.[16]

Second, in her season of deep mourning, the Lord gave her purpose. Emma didn't just have a front-row seat to the Restoration; she was an essential participant in the work taking place. She would be set apart "to expound scriptures, and to exhort the church."[17] Her time would "be given to writing, and to learning much."[18] Emma was given a sacred role to help prepare the Saints to worship; their songs unto the Lord would be received as prayers and "answered with a blessing upon their heads."[19]

Last, the Lord outlined a process of inward sanctification[20] that would prepare Emma for exaltation. "Except thou do this," the Lord explained to her, "where I am you cannot come."[21]

If we read section 25 carefully, we discover an important progression taking place. Emma would go from being a daughter in the kingdom[22] to "elect lady"[23] to queen.[24] Aaronic and Melchizedek Priesthood ordinances, combined with the keeping of her covenant promises, would increase her companionship with the Spirit and with angels, empowering her to navigate her life with divine guidance.[25] Through His divine power, God would heal her heart, enlarge her capacity, and transform her into the version of herself He knew she could become. And through the ordinances of the Melchizedek Priesthood, "the power of godliness [would be] manifest"[26] in her life, and the Lord would part the veil so she could receive understanding from Him.[27] *This* is what it looks like for God's power to work within us.

President Russell M. Nelson taught:

"*Everything* that happened in [Harmony] has profound implications for *your* lives. The restoration of the priesthood, along with the Lord's counsel to Emma, can guide and bless each of you. . . .

" . . . Accessing the power of God in your life requires the same things that the Lord instructed Emma and each of [us] to do."[28]

There were important things happening on both sides of that window in Harmony, including the revelation given to the elect lady whom the Lord had called—a revelation that would strengthen, encourage, and instruct Emma Smith, God's daughter.[29]

When our granddaughter Isabelle was given a name and a blessing, her father blessed her with an understanding of the priesthood; that she would continue to grow in and learn about the blessing it would provide in her life; and that her faith in the priesthood would grow as she continued to grow in understanding.

It is not often a little girl is blessed to understand the priesthood and to learn how those priesthood ordinances and covenant promises will help her to access God's power. But I remembered Emma and thought to myself, Why not? This tiny daughter has the potential to become an elect lady in His kingdom and eventually a queen. Through His priesthood ordinances and the keeping of her covenant promises, God's power will work in and through her to help her overcome whatever life brings and become the woman God knows she can become. This is something I want each girl in the kingdom to understand.

"Live up to your privileges."[30]

Learn how priesthood ordinances and covenant promises will allow God's power to flow into your life with greater efficacy, working in and through you, empowering and equipping you to reach your full purpose and potential.

Carefully study and ponder the Aaronic and the Melchizedek

Priesthood ordinances, the covenant promises we make with each, and the power of God we access through those ordinances.[31]

Remember, it's not only who officiates in the ordinance that matters; what the ordinance and your covenant promise unlock also deserves the focus of your attention.

Partaking of the bread and water is a weekly reminder of His power working in you to help you overcome. Wearing the garment of the holy priesthood is a daily reminder of the gift of His power working in you to help you become.

We all have access to the gift of God's power.

Every time we partake of the sacrament.

Every time we cross the threshold of a temple.[32]

This is the highlight of my Sabbath. This is why I cherish my temple recommend.

"In the ordinances thereof, the power of godliness is manifest."[33]

Of this gift I bear witness in the name of Jesus Christ, amen.

Notes

1. See Doctrine and Covenants 107:20.
2. Elder D. Todd Christofferson taught: "In all the ordinances, especially those of the temple, we are endowed with power from on high. This 'power of godliness' comes in the person and by the influence of the Holy Ghost. . . . I testify that God will keep His promises to you as you honor your covenants with Him. . . . He will, by His Holy Spirit, fill you with godly power" ("The Power of Covenants," *Ensign* or *Liahona*, May 2009, 22, 23).
3. See Dallin H. Oaks, "The Aaronic Priesthood and the Sacrament," *Ensign*, Nov. 1998, 39; *Liahona*, Jan. 1999, 45.
4. "Every man and every woman who participates in priesthood ordinances and who makes and keeps covenants with God has direct access to the power of God" (Russell M. Nelson, "The Everlasting Covenant," *Liahona*, Oct. 2022, 10).
5. See Joshua 3:5, footnote *a*. Elder Dale G. Renlund explained: "Through these covenants, we have greater access to [the Lord's] power. To be clear, baptismal and temple covenants are not, in and of themselves, the source of power. The source of power is the Lord Jesus Christ and our Heavenly Father. Making and keeping covenants create a conduit for Their power in our lives." ("The Powerful, Virtuous Cycle of the Doctrine of Christ," *Liahona*, May 2024, 82.)
6. See Doctrine and Covenants 107:1–3; Joseph Smith Translation, Hebrews 7:3 (in the Bible appendix); Alma 13:2, 16. President Dallin H. Oaks taught: "From the scriptures we also know that those who officiate in the priesthood act in behalf of the Lord (see Doctrine and Covenants 1:38; 36:2). I will now suggest how teachers and priests and deacons should carry out their sacred responsibilities to act in behalf of the Lord in preparing, administering, and passing the sacrament" ("The Aaronic Priesthood and the Sacrament," *Ensign*, Nov. 1998, 39; *Liahona*, Jan. 1999, 45).
7. See *General Handbook: Serving in The Church of Jesus Christ of Latter-day Saints*, 3.5.1–2, Gospel Library.
8. See Doctrine and Covenants 107:18–20; Philippians 1:6.
9. See Russell M. Nelson, "Spiritual Treasures," *Ensign* or *Liahona*, Nov. 2019, 77.
10. See "Joseph and Emma Smith's Home" (history.ChurchofJesusChrist.org) for more detail about the reproduction of the Smith home at the Church historic site in Harmony, Pennsylvania.

11. The authority and keys of the priesthood allow God's power to flow into the lives of those who receive priesthood ordinances and make and keep the associated covenants (see *General Handbook*, 3.5, Gospel Library).

12. See Joseph Smith—History 1:71, note.

13. See Doctrine and Covenants 25.

14. See Doctrine and Covenants 25:1.

15. Doctrine and Covenants 25:2.

16. See Doctrine and Covenants 25:13. "The word *covenant* is of Latin origin, *con venire*, and literally means a 'coming together.' In the context of the priesthood, a 'covenant' is a coming together or an agreement between God and man. It presupposes that God and man come together to make a contract, to agree on promises, stipulations, privileges, and responsibilities. . . .

   "A covenant made in this manner is immutable and unchangeable. It anchors the soul; it creates a steadfast and sure foundation for future expectations" (Dale G. Renlund and Ruth Lybbert Renlund, *The Melchizedek Priesthood: Understanding the Doctrine, Living the Principles* [2018], 60).

17. Doctrine and Covenants 25:7.

18. Doctrine and Covenants 25:8.

19. Doctrine and Covenants 25:12.

20. See Doctrine and Covenants 25:15.

21. Doctrine and Covenants 25:15. President Dallin H. Oaks taught: "The ordinance of baptism and its associated covenants are requirements for entrance into the celestial kingdom. The ordinances and associated covenants of the temple are requirements for exaltation in the celestial kingdom, which is eternal life, 'the greatest of all the gifts of God' [Doctrine and Covenants 14:7]" ("Covenants and Responsibilities," *Liahona*, May 2024, 96).

22. See Doctrine and Covenants 25:1.

23. Doctrine and Covenants 25:3.

24. See Doctrine and Covenants 25:15.

25. See Dallin H. Oaks, "The Aaronic Priesthood and the Sacrament," *Ensign*, Nov. 1998, 38–39; *Liahona*, Jan. 1999, 44–45. President Oaks taught:
   "In a closely related way, these ordinances of the Aaronic Priesthood are also vital to the ministering of angels. . . .
   " . . . Angelic messages can be delivered by a voice or merely by thoughts or feelings communicated to the mind" ("The Aaronic Priesthood and the Sacrament," *Ensign*, Nov. 1998, 38, 39; *Liahona*, Jan. 1999, 44, 45).
   In addition, the Prophet Joseph Smith gave this promise when speaking to Relief Society sisters: "If you live up to your privileges, the angels cannot be restrained from being your associates" (*Teachings of Presidents of the Church: Joseph Smith* [2011], 454).

26. See Doctrine and Covenants 84:19–20.

27. See Doctrine and Covenants 107:18–19.

28. Russell M. Nelson, "Spiritual Treasures," 77. "*Willard Richards reported:* 'President Joseph Smith read the revelation [given] to Emma Smith . . . and stated that . . . not she alone, but others, may attain to the same blessings'" (*Teachings: Joseph Smith*, 453–54). See also Nauvoo Relief Society Minute Book, March 17, 1842, in *The First Fifty Years of Relief Society: Key Documents in Latter-day Saint Women's History* (2016), 1.2.1, churchhistorianspress.org.

29. See Doctrine and Covenants 24, section heading. This states that "the following three revelations were given at this time to strengthen, encourage, and instruct."

30. *Teachings: Joseph Smith*, 454.

31. See Russell M. Nelson, "Spiritual Treasures," 77. "I entreat you to study prayerfully *all* the truths you can find about priesthood power. You might begin with Doctrine and Covenants sections 84 and 107. Those sections will lead you to other passages. The scriptures and teachings by modern prophets, seers, and revelators are filled with these truths. As your understanding increases and as you exercise faith in the Lord and His priesthood power, your ability to draw upon this spiritual treasure that the Lord has made available will increase" (Russell M. Nelson, "Spiritual Treasures," 79).

32. See Doctrine and Covenants 109:22.

33. Doctrine and Covenants 84:20.

GOD'S FAVOURITE

ELDER KARL D. HIRST
Of the Seventy

Before I begin, I should tell you that two of my children have passed out whilst speaking at pulpits, and I have never felt more connected to them than in this moment. I've got more on my mind than just the trapdoor.

Our family has six children, who sometimes tease one another that they are the favourite child. Each has different reasons for being preferred. Our love for each of our children is pure and fulfilling and complete. We could not love any one of them any more than another—with each child's birth came the most beautiful expansion of our love. I most relate to my Heavenly Father's love for me through the love that I feel for my children.

As they each rehearse their claims to be the most loved child, you might have thought that our family had never had an untidy bedroom. The sense of blemishes in the relationship between parent and child is diminished with a focus on love.

At some point, perhaps because I can see that we are heading toward an inevitable family riot, I'll say something like, "OK, you have worn me down, but I am not going to announce it; you know which one of you is my favourite." My goal is that each one of the six feels victorious and all-out war is avoided—at least until next time!

In his Gospel, John describes himself as "the disciple whom Jesus loved,"[1] as if that arrangement were somehow unique. I like to think that this was because John felt so completely loved by Jesus. Nephi gave me a similar sense when he wrote, "I glory in *my* Jesus."[2] Of course, the Saviour isn't Nephi's any more than He is John's, and yet the personal nature of Nephi's relationship with "his" Jesus led him to that tender description.

Isn't it wonderful that there are times when we can feel so fully and personally noticed and loved? Nephi can call Him "his" Jesus, and so can we. Our Saviour's love is the "highest, noblest, strongest kind of love,"[3] and He provides until we are "filled."[4] Divine love never runs dry, and we are each a cherished favourite. God's love is where, as circles on a Venn diagram, we all overlap. Whichever parts of us seem different, His love is where we find togetherness.

Is it any surprise that the greatest commandments are to love God and to love those around us?[5] When I see people showing Christlike love for one another, it feels to me as if that love contains more than just *their* love; it is love that also has divinity in it.[6] When we love one another in this way, as completely and fully as we can, heaven gets involved too.[7]

So if someone we care about seems distant from a sense of divine love, we can follow this pattern—by doing things that bring us closer to God ourselves and then doing things that bring us closer to them—an unspoken beckoning to come to Christ.

I wish I could sit down with you and ask you what circumstances cause you to feel God's love. Which verses of scripture, which particular acts of service? Where would you be? What music? In whose company? General conference is a rich place to learn about connecting with heaven's love.

But perhaps you feel a long way from the love of God. Maybe there is a chorus of voices of discouragement and darkness that weighs into your thoughts, messages telling you that you are too wounded and confused, too weak and overlooked, too different or disoriented to warrant heavenly love in any real way. If you hear those ideas, then please hear this: those voices are just wrong. We can confidently disregard brokenness in any way disqualifying us from heavenly love—every time we sing the hymn that reminds us that our beloved and flawless Saviour chose to be "bruised, broken, [and] torn for us,"[8] every time we take broken bread. Surely Jesus removes all shame from the broken. Through His brokenness, He became perfect, and He can make us perfect in spite of our brokenness.[9] Broken, lonely, torn, and bruised He was—and we may feel we are—but separated from the love of God we are not. "Broken people, perfect love,"[10] as the song goes.

You might know something secret about yourself that makes

you feel unlovable. However right you might be about what you know about yourself, you are wrong to think that you have put yourself beyond the reach of God's love. We are sometimes cruel and impatient toward ourselves in ways that we could never imagine being toward anyone else. There is much for us to do in this life, but self-loathing and shameful self-condemnation are not on that list. However misshapen *we* might feel *we* are, *His* arms are not shortened.[11] No. They are always long enough to "[reach our] reaching"[12] and embrace each one of us.

When we don't feel the warmth of divine love, it hasn't gone away. God's own words are that "the mountains shall depart, and the hills be removed; but [His] kindness shall not depart from [us]."[13] So, just to be clear, the idea that God has stopped loving should be so far down the list of possible explanations in life that we don't get to it until after the mountains have left and the hills are gone!

I really enjoy this symbolism of mountains being evidence of the certainty of God's love. That powerful symbolism weaves into accounts of those who go to the mountains to receive revelation[14] and Isaiah's description of "the mountain of the Lord's house" being "established in the top of the mountains."[15] The house of the Lord is the home of our most precious covenants and a place for us all to retreat[16] and sink deeply into the evidence of our Father's love for us.[17] I have also enjoyed the comfort that comes to my soul when I wrap myself more tightly in my baptismal covenant and find someone who is mourning a loss or grieving a disappointment and I try to help them hold and process their feelings.[18] Are these ways that we can become more immersed in the precious covenantal love *hesed*?[19]

So if God's love does not leave us, why don't we always feel it? Just to manage your expectations: I don't know. But *being* loved is definitely not the same as *feeling* loved, and I have a few thoughts that might help you as you pursue your answers to that question.

Perhaps you are wrestling with grief, depression, betrayal, loneliness, disappointment, or other powerful intrusion into your ability to feel God's love for you. If so, these things can dull or suspend our ability to feel as we might otherwise feel. For a season at least, perhaps you will not be able to *feel* His love, and knowledge will have to suffice. But I wonder if you could experiment—patiently—with different ways of expressing and receiving divine love. Can you take a step back from whatever is in front of you and maybe another step and another, until you see a wider landscape, wider and wider still if necessary, until you are literally "thinking celestial"[20] because you are looking at the stars and remembering worlds without number and through them their Creator?

Birdsong, feeling the sun or a breeze or rain on my skin, and times when nature puts my senses in awe of God—each has had a part in providing me with heavenly connection. Perhaps the comfort of faithful friends will help. Maybe music? Or serving? Have you kept a record or journal of times when your connection with God was clearer to you? Perhaps you could invite those you trust to share their sources of divine connection with you as you search for relief and understanding.

I wonder, if Jesus were to choose a place where you and He could meet, a private place where you would be able to have a singular focus on Him, might He choose your unique place of personal suffering, the place of your deepest need, where no one else can go? Somewhere you feel so lonely that you must truly be all alone but you aren't quite, a place to which perhaps only He has travelled but actually has already prepared to meet you there when you arrive? If you are waiting for Him to come, might He already be there and within reach?

If you do feel filled with love in this season of your life, please try and hold on to it as effectively as a sieve holds water. Splash it everywhere you go. One of the miracles of the divine economy is that when we try to share Jesus's love, we find ourselves being filled up in a variation of the principle that "whosoever will lose his life for my sake shall find it."[21]

Being filled with God's love shields us in life's storms but also makes the happy moments happier—our joyful days, when there is sunshine in the sky, are made even brighter by the sunshine in our souls.

Let's become "rooted and grounded"[22] in our Jesus and in His love. Let's look for and treasure experiences of feeling His love and power in our lives. The joy of the gospel is available to all: not just the happy, not just the downcast. Joy is our purpose, not the gift of our circumstances. We have every good reason to "rejoice and be filled with love towards God and all men."[24] Let's get full.[25] In the name of Jesus Christ, amen.

Notes

1. John 21:20; see also John 13:23; 19:26; 20:2; 21:7.
2. 2 Nephi 33:6; emphasis added.
3. Bible Dictionary, "Charity."
4. In the Holy Land: Matthew 14:15–20. And in the Americas: 3 Nephi 27:16.
5. See Matthew 22:35–40.
6. See 1 John 4:12.
7. *For the Strength of Youth: A Guide for Making Choices* asks that we "help [others] feel Heavenly Father's love through [us]" ([2022], 12).
8. "Jesus of Nazareth, Savior and King," *Hymns*, no. 181; see also Isaiah 53:5; Matthew 26:26.
9. President Russell M. Nelson explained: "Just prior to [the Savior's] crucifixion, He said that on 'the third day I *shall be perfected*' [Luke 13:32; emphasis added]. Think of that! The sinless, errorless Lord—already perfect by our mortal standards—proclaimed his own state of perfection yet to be in the future. His *eternal* perfection would follow his resurrection and receipt of 'all power . . . in heaven and in earth' [Matthew 28:18; see also Doctrine and Covenants 93:2–23]" ("Perfection Pending," *Ensign*, Nov. 1995, 87). The prophet Moroni invited all to "come unto Christ, and be perfected in him, and deny yourselves of all ungodliness; and if ye shall deny yourselves of all ungodliness, and love God with all your might, mind and strength, then is his grace sufficient for you, that by his grace ye may be perfect in Christ" (Moroni 10:32).
10. "Savior of My Soul," *2024 Youth Album*, ChurchofJesusChrist.org.
11. See Isaiah 59:1.
12. "Where Can I Turn for Peace?," *Hymns*, no. 129.
13. Isaiah 54:10.
14. For example, Nephi (see 1 Nephi 17:7), Moses (see Exodus 19:3), the eleven disciples (see Matthew 28:16), and the Saviour (see Matthew 14:23); see also Psalm 24:3.
15. Isaiah 2:2; see also verse 3. This symbolism causes me to consider further the Lord's purposes in providing hundreds of temples for His children throughout the world.
16. My experience bears out the truth of President Nelson's promise that the safest place to be living is inside our temple covenants (see "The Temple and Your Spiritual Foundation," *Liahona*, Nov. 2021, 96).
17. President Nelson has assured us:
    "Time in the temple will help you to *think celestial* and to catch a vision of who you really are, who you can become, and the kind of life you can have forever. Regular temple worship will enhance the way you see yourself and how you fit into God's magnificent plan. I promise you that. . . .
    " . . . Nothing will soothe your spirit *more* during times of pain. Nothing will open the heavens *more*. Nothing!" ("Rejoice in the Gift of Priesthood Keys," *Liahona*, May 2024, 121, 122).
18. See Mosiah 18:8–10, 13. "The baptismal covenant is a public witness to Heavenly Father of three specific commitments: to serve God, to keep His commandments, and to be willing to take on the name of Jesus Christ. The other facets that are frequently associated with the baptismal covenant—that we 'bear one another's burdens,' 'mourn with those that mourn,' and 'comfort those that [are] in need of comfort' [Mosiah 18:8, 9]—are fruits of making the covenant rather than part of the actual covenant. These facets are important because they are what a converted soul would naturally do" (Dale G. Renlund, "Stronger and Closer Connection

to God through Multiple Covenants" [Brigham Young University devotional, Mar. 5, 2024], speeches.byu.edu).

19. See Russell M. Nelson, "The Everlasting Covenant," *Liahona*, Oct. 2022, 4–11.
20. See Russell M. Nelson "Think Celestial!," *Liahona*, Nov. 2023, 117, 118.
21. Matthew 16:25.
22. Ephesians 3:17.
23. See 2 Nephi 2:25; Russell M. Nelson, "Joy and Spiritual Survival," *Ensign* or *Liahona*, Nov. 2016, 81–84.
24. Mosiah 2:4.
25. See Moroni 7:48.

"THIS IS MY GOSPEL"— "THIS IS MY CHURCH"

ELDER DALE G. RENLUND
Of the Quorum of the Twelve Apostles

For centuries, black powder was the most powerful explosive available.[1] It could launch cannon balls, but it wasn't effective for most mining and road construction projects. It was just too weak to shatter rock.

In 1846 an Italian chemist named Ascanio Sobrero synthesized a new explosive, nitroglycerin. This oily fluid was at least a thousand times more powerful than black powder. It could easily shatter rock. Unfortunately, nitroglycerin was unstable. If you dropped it from a small height, it'd blow up. If it got too hot, it'd blow up. If it got too cold, it'd blow up. Even placed in a cool, dark room and left alone, it'd eventually blow up. Most countries banned its transportation, and many banned its manufacture.

In 1860 a Swedish scientist named Alfred Nobel began trying to stabilize nitroglycerin. After seven years of experimentation, he achieved his goal by absorbing nitroglycerin into a nearly worthless substance known as diatomaceous earth, or kieselguhr. Kieselguhr is a porous rock that can be crumbled into a fine powder. When mixed with nitroglycerin, kieselguhr absorbs the nitroglycerin, and the resultant paste can be shaped into "sticks." In this form, nitroglycerin was much more stable. It could be safely stored, transported, and used with undiminished explosive power. Nobel named the combination of nitroglycerin and kieselguhr "dynamite."

Dynamite changed the world. It also made Nobel wealthy.[2] Without a stabilizer, nitroglycerin was just too hazardous to be commercially valuable, as Ascanio Sobrero found out.[3] By itself, as I mentioned, kieselguhr was of little value.[4] But the combination of the two components made dynamite transformative and precious.

In a similar way, the combination of the gospel of Jesus Christ[5] and The Church of Jesus Christ of Latter-day Saints provides powerful and transformative benefits for us. The gospel is perfect, but a divinely commissioned church is required to preach it, maintain its purity, and administer its sacred ordinances with the Savior's power and authority.

Consider the combination of the Savior's gospel and His Church as established by the Book of Mormon prophet Alma. The Church was responsible for preaching "nothing save it were repentance and faith on the Lord, who [would redeem] his people."[6] Using God's authority, the Church was responsible for administering the ordinance of baptism "in the name of the Lord, as a witness [of entering] into a covenant with him [to] serve him and keep his commandments."[7] The people who were baptized took on themselves the name of Jesus Christ,[8] joined His Church,[9] and were promised great power through an outpouring of the Spirit.[10]

People flocked to the Waters of Mormon to hear Alma preach the gospel. Though they revered those waters and the surrounding forests, the Lord's Church was not a location or a building, nor is it today. The Church is simply ordinary people, disciples of Jesus Christ, gathered and organized into a divinely appointed structure that helps the Lord accomplish His purposes. The Church is the instrument through which we learn the central role of Jesus Christ in Heavenly Father's plan. The Church offers the authoritative way for individuals to participate in ordinances and make lasting covenants with God.[11] Keeping those covenants draws us closer to God, gives us access to His power,[12] and transforms us into who He intends us to become.[13]

Just as dynamite without nitroglycerin is unremarkable, the Savior's Church is special only if it is built on His gospel.[14] Without the Savior's gospel and the authority to administer the ordinances thereof,[15] the Church isn't exceptional.[16]

Without the stabilizing effect of kieselguhr, nitroglycerin had limited value as an explosive. As history has shown, without the Lord's Church, humanity's understanding of His gospel was likewise unstable—prone to doctrinal drift and subject to the influence of different religions, cultures, and philosophies.[17] An amalgamation of those influences has been manifested in every dispensation leading up to this last one.[18] Though the gospel was initially revealed in its purity, the interpretation and application of that gospel gradually took on a form of godliness that lacked power because the divinely authorized framework was absent.[19]

The Church of Jesus Christ of Latter-day Saints enables access to God's power because it is authorized by Him both to teach the doctrine of Christ and to offer the gospel's saving and exalting ordinances.[20] The Savior yearns to forgive our sins, help us access His power, and transform us.[21] He suffered for our sins and longs to pardon us from the punishment that we otherwise would deserve.[22] He wants us to become holy[23] and be perfected in Him.[24]

Jesus Christ has the power to do this. He didn't simply sympathize with our imperfections[25] and lament our eternal condemnation in consequence of sin.[26] No, He went beyond that, infinitely beyond that, and restored His Church to enable access to His power.

The core of the gospel that the Church teaches is that Jesus Christ bore "our griefs, and carried our sorrows." He had "laid on him the iniquity of us all."[27] He "endured the cross,"[28] broke "the bands of death,"[29] "ascended into heaven, and . . . sat down on the right hand of God, to claim of the Father his rights of mercy." The Savior did all this because He loves His Father and He loves us. He has already paid the infinite price so He can "[claim] all those who have faith in him [and advocate]"[30] for them—for us. Jesus Christ wants nothing more than for us to repent and come unto Him so that He can justify and sanctify us. In this desire, He is relentless and unwavering.

The access to God's covenantal power and His covenantal love is through His Church. The combination of the Savior's gospel and His Church transforms our lives. It transformed my maternal grandparents. My grandfather Oskar Andersson worked in a shipyard on Högmarsö, an island in the Stockholm archipelago. His wife, Albertina, and their children lived on the Swedish mainland. Once every two weeks, on Saturday, Oskar rowed his boat home for the weekend before returning to Högmarsö on Sunday evening. One day, while on Högmarsö, he heard two American missionaries preach the restored gospel of Jesus Christ. Oskar felt that what he heard was pure truth, and he was filled with unspeakable joy.

The next time he returned home, Oskar excitedly told Albertina all about the missionaries. He explained that he believed what they taught. He asked her to read the pamphlets they had given him, and he told her that he didn't think that any of their future children should be baptized as infants. Albertina was furious and threw the pamphlets on the rubbish heap. Not much was said between them before Oskar returned to work on Sunday evening.

As soon as he was gone, Albertina retrieved those pamphlets. She carefully compared their doctrine with the teachings in her well-worn Bible. She was astonished to feel that what she read was true. The next time Oskar returned home, he received a warm welcome, as did the copy of the Book of Mormon he brought with him. Albertina eagerly read, again comparing the doctrine to that in her Bible. Like Oskar, she recognized pure truth and was filled with unspeakable joy.

Oskar, Albertina, and their children moved to Högmarsö to be close to the few Church members there. A week after Oskar and Albertina were baptized in 1916, Oskar was called to be the group leader on Högmarsö. Like many converts, Oskar and Albertina faced criticism because of their new faith. Local farmers refused to sell them milk, so Oskar rowed across the fjord every day to purchase milk from a more tolerant farmer.

Yet during the ensuing years, Church membership on Högmarsö increased, in part because of Albertina's powerful testimony and burning missionary zeal. When the group became a branch, Oskar was called as the branch president.

Members of that Högmarsö branch revered that island. This was their Waters of Mormon.[31] This was where they came to a knowledge of their Redeemer.

Over the years, as they kept their baptismal covenant, Oskar and Albertina were transformed by the power of Jesus Christ. They longed to make more covenants and receive their temple blessings. To obtain those blessings, they permanently emigrated from their home in Sweden to Salt Lake City in 1949. Oskar had served as the leader of the members on Högmarsö for 33 years.[32]

The combination of nitroglycerin and kieselguhr made dynamite valuable; the combination of the gospel of Jesus Christ and His Church is beyond price. Oskar and Albertina heard about the restored gospel because a prophet of God had called, assigned, and sent missionaries to Sweden. By divine commission, missionaries taught the doctrine of Christ and by priesthood authority baptized Oskar and Albertina. As members, Oskar and Albertina continued learning, developing, and serving others. They became Latter-day Saints because they kept the covenants they made.

The Savior refers to The Church of Jesus Christ of Latter-day Saints as "my church" because He commissioned it to accomplish His purposes[33]—preaching His gospel, offering His ordinances and covenants, and making it possible for His power to justify and sanctify us. Without His Church, there is no authority, no preaching of revealed truths in His name, no ordinances or covenants, no manifestation of the power of godliness,[34] no transformation into who God wants us to become, and God's plan for His children is set at naught. The Church in this dispensation is integral to His plan.[35]

I invite you to commit yourself more fully to the Savior, His gospel, and His Church. As you do so, you will find that the combination of the Savior's gospel and His Church brings power into your life. This power is far greater than dynamite. It'll shatter the rocks in your way, transform you into an inheritor in God's kingdom. And you will be "filled with that joy which is unspeakable and full of glory."[36] In the name of Jesus Christ, amen.

Notes

1. Black powder is a mixture of potassium nitrate (saltpeter), sulfur, and charcoal. It is classified as a *low explosive* or a *low-yield explosive* because of its relatively slow decomposition rate, burning at subsonic speeds. *High explosives* or *high-yield explosives* detonate rather than burn, producing a supersonic shock wave.
2. Dynamite enabled "an unprecedented surge in the creation of rail tunnels, sewer systems, and subways around the world—major engineering projects that would have been impossible to [accomplish] without the controlled explosions [that it allowed]. Almost all the iconic engineering triumphs of the [late 19th and early 20th centuries]—the London Underground, the Brooklyn Bridge, the Transcontinental Railroad, [and] the Panama Canal—relied extensively on the new explosive" (Steven Johnson, *The Infernal Machine: A True Story of Dynamite, Terror, and the Rise of the Modern Detective* [2024], 24).
3. Because nitroglycerin itself was not commercially viable, Ascanio Sobrero did not become wealthy because of his invention. However, when Alfred Nobel built a dynamite factory at Avigliana, Italy, in 1873, Sobrero was appointed as a well-paid adviser in recognition of his

discovery of nitroglycerin. Sobrero held that appointment until his death in 1888. (See G. I. Brown, *The Big Bang: A History of Explosives* [1998], 106.)

4. For the history of black powder, nitroglycerin, and dynamite, see Brown, *The Big Bang*, 1–121.

5. The gospel of Jesus Christ is synonymous with the doctrine of Christ.

6. See Mosiah 18:7, 20; 25:15, 22.

7. Mosiah 18:10.

8. See 2 Nephi 31:13.

9. See Mosiah 18:17; 25:18, 23; Alma 4:4–5; Helaman 3:24–26; 3 Nephi 28:18, 23.

10. See 2 Nephi 31:12–14; Mosiah 18:10.

11. The Church is key to offering sacred covenants to Heavenly Father's children. This is why, during the endowment in temples, members covenant to keep the law of consecration. This means that they "dedicate their time, talents, and everything with which the Lord has blessed them to building up Jesus Christ's Church on the earth" (*General Handbook: Serving in The Church of Jesus Christ of Latter-day Saints*, 27.2, Gospel Library).

12. See Russell M. Nelson, "Spiritual Treasures," *Ensign* or *Liahona*, Nov. 2019, 77.

13. See Mosiah 18:22; Moses 6:68; Guide to the Scriptures, "Sons and Daughters of God," Gospel Library.

14. See 3 Nephi 27:13–21.

15. See Articles of Faith 1:5.

16. See Russell M. Nelson, "Rejoice in the Gift of Priesthood Keys," *Liahona*, May 2024, 121; 3 Nephi 27:9–11.

17. The Savior "gave some, apostles; and some, prophets; and some, evangelists; and some, pastors and teachers" so that "we [could] all come in the unity of the faith, and of the knowledge of the Son of God, . . . that we henceforth be no more children, tossed to and fro, and carried about with every wind of doctrine, by the sleight of men, and cunning craftiness, whereby they lie in wait to deceive" (Ephesians 4:11, 13–14).

18. *Syncretism* is the technical term for the amalgamation of different religions, cultures, or schools of thought.

19. See Joseph Smith—History 1:19.

20. See "The Restoration of the Fulness of the Gospel of Jesus Christ: A Bicentennial Proclamation to the World," Gospel Library. The proclamation was read by President Russell M. Nelson as part of his message at the 190th Annual General Conference, April 5, 2020, in Salt Lake City, Utah (see "Hear Him," *Ensign* or *Liahona*, May 2020, 91–92).

21. We can access God's power by exercising faith in Jesus Christ, repenting of our sins, and keeping the covenants we make with Heavenly Father and Jesus Christ in ordinances such as baptism, the endowment, and the sacrament.

22. See Guide to the Scriptures, "Justification, Justify," Gospel Library.

23. See Guide to the Scriptures, "Sanctification," Gospel Library.

24. See Moroni 10:32–33.

25. See Hebrews 4:15; see also footnote *a*.

26. See Doctrine and Covenants 19:15–18.

27. See Isaiah 53:4–12.

28. Hebrews 12:2.

29. Mosiah 15:23.

30. Moroni 7:27–28; see also Doctrine and Covenants 45:3–5.

31. See Mosiah 18:30.

32. See Inger Höglund and Caj-Aage Johansson, *Steg i Tro: Jesu Kristi Kyrka av Sista Dagars Heliga i Sverige 1850–2000* (2000), 66–67.

33. Doctrine and Covenants 115:4.

34. See Doctrine and Covenants 84:19–21.

35. If you receive what the Lord's Church offers, you can be perfected in Christ before His Church is perfected, if it ever is. His goal is to perfect you, not His Church. His goal has never been to, metaphorically, turn kieselguhr into diamond; His goal has been to refine you into pure gold, to save and exalt you as a co-inheritor with Him in the kingdom of our Heavenly Father. But that needs to become your goal, too. It is your choice.

36. Helaman 5:44.

TRUSTING OUR FATHER

ELDER DAVID P. HOMER
Of the Seventy

On June 1, 1843, Addison Pratt left Nauvoo, Illinois, to preach the gospel in the Hawaiian Islands, leaving his wife, Louisa Barnes Pratt, to care for their young family.

In Nauvoo, as persecutions intensified, forcing the Saints to leave, and later at Winter Quarters as they prepared to migrate to the Salt Lake Valley, Louisa faced the decision of whether to make the journey. It would have been easier to stay and to wait for Addison to return than to travel alone.

On both occasions, she sought guidance from the prophet, Brigham Young, who encouraged her to go. Despite the great difficulty and her personal reluctance, she successfully made the journey each time.

Initially, Louisa found little joy in traveling. However, she soon began to welcome the green prairie grass, colorful wildflowers, and patches of ground along the riverbanks. "The gloom on my mind wore gradually away," she recorded, "and there was not a more mirthful woman in the whole company."[1]

Louisa's story has deeply inspired me. I admire her willingness to set aside her personal preferences, her ability to trust God, and how exercising her faith helped her to see the situation differently.

She has reminded me that we have a loving Father in Heaven, who cares for us wherever we are, and that we can trust Him more than anyone or anything else.[2]

The Source of Truth

God trusts us to make many important decisions, and in all matters He asks us to trust Him.[3] This is especially difficult when our judgment or public opinion differs from His will for His children.

Some suggest that we should redraw the lines between what is right and what is wrong because they say that truth is relative, reality is self-defined, or God is so generous that He does not actually care about what we do.

As we seek to understand and accept God's will, it is helpful to remember that the boundaries between right and wrong are not for us to define. God has established these boundaries Himself, based on eternal truths for our benefit and blessing.

The desire to change God's eternal truth has a long history. It started before the world began, when Satan rebelled against God's plan, seeking selfishly to destroy human agency.[4] Following this pattern, people like Sherem, Nehor, and Korihor have argued that faith is foolish, revelation is irrelevant, and whatever we want to do is right.[5] Sadly, so very often these deviations from God's truth have led to great sorrow.

While some things may depend on context, not everything does. President Russell M. Nelson has consistently taught that God's saving truths are absolute, independent, and defined by God Himself.[6]

Our Choice

Whom we choose to trust is one of life's important decisions. King Benjamin instructed his people, "Believe in God; believe that he is . . . ; believe that he has all wisdom . . . ; believe that man doth not comprehend all the things which the Lord can comprehend."[7]

Fortunately, we have the scriptures and guidance from living prophets to help us understand God's truth. If clarification beyond what we have is needed, God provides it through His prophets. And He will respond to our sincere prayers through the Holy Ghost as we seek to understand truths we do not yet fully appreciate.

Elder Neil L. Andersen once taught that we should not be surprised "if at times [our] personal views are not initially in harmony with the teachings of the Lord's prophet. These are moments of learning," he said, "of humility, when we go to our knees in prayer. We walk forward in faith, trusting in God, knowing that with time we will receive more spiritual clarity from our Heavenly Father."[8]

At all times, it is helpful to remember Alma's teaching that God gives His word according to the attention and effort we devote to it. If we heed God's word, we will receive more; if we ignore His counsel, we will receive less and less until we have none.[9] This loss of knowledge does not mean that the truth was wrong; rather, it shows that we have lost the capacity to understand it.[10]

Look to the Savior

In Capernaum, the Savior taught about His identity and mission. Many found His words difficult to hear, leading them to turn their backs and "[walk] no more with him."[11]

Why did they walk away?

Because they did not like what He said. So, trusting their own judgment, they walked away, denying themselves blessings that would have come had they stayed.

It is easy for our pride to come between us and eternal truth. When we don't understand, we can pause, let our feelings settle, and then choose how to respond. The Savior urged us to "look unto [Him] in every thought; doubt not, fear not."[12] When we focus on the Savior, our faith can start to overcome our concerns.

As President Dieter F. Uchtdorf encouraged us to do: "Please, first doubt your doubts before you doubt your faith. We must never allow doubt to hold us prisoner and keep us from the divine love, peace, and gifts that come through faith in the Lord Jesus Christ."[13]

Blessings Come to Those Who Stay

As the disciples walked away from the Savior that day, He then asked the Twelve, "Will ye also go away?"

Peter answered:

"Lord, to whom shall we go? thou hast the words of eternal life.

"And we believe and are sure that thou art that Christ, the Son of the living God."[14]

Now, the Apostles lived in the same world, and they faced the same social pressures as the disciples who walked away. However, in this moment, they chose their faith and trusted God, thus preserving blessings God gives to those who stay.

Perhaps you, like me, sometimes find yourself on both sides of this decision. When we find it difficult to understand or embrace God's will, it is comforting to remember that He loves us as we are, wherever we are. And He has something better for us. If we reach out to Him, He will assist us.

While reaching out to Him can be difficult, just as the father who sought healing for his son was told by the Savior, "All things are possible to him that believeth."[15] In our moments of struggle, we too can cry out, "Help thou [my] unbelief."[16]

Submitting Our Will to His

Elder Neal A. Maxwell once taught that "the submission of one's will is really the only uniquely personal thing we have to place on God's altar."[17] No wonder King Benjamin was so eager that his people become "as a child, submissive, meek, humble, patient, full of love, willing to submit to all things which the Lord seeth fit to inflict upon him, even as a child doth submit to his father."[18]

As always, the Savior set the perfect example for us. With a heavy heart, and knowing the painful work He had to do, He submitted to His Father's will, fulfilling His messianic mission and opening the promise of eternity to you and me.[19]

The choice to submit our will to God's is an act of faith that lies at the heart of our discipleship. In making that choice, we discover that our agency is not diminished; rather, it is magnified and rewarded by the presence of the Holy Ghost, who brings purpose, joy, peace, and hope we can find nowhere else.[20]

Several months ago, a stake president and I visited a sister in his stake and her young adult son. After years away from the Church, wandering difficult and unfriendly paths, she had returned. During our visit, we asked her why she had come back.

"I had made a mess of my life," she said, "and I knew where I needed to be."

I then asked her what she had learned in her journey.

With some emotion, she shared that she had learned that she needed to attend church long enough to break the habit of not coming and that she needed to stay until it was where she wanted to be. Her return was not easy, but as she exercised faith in the Father's plan, she felt the Spirit return.

And then she added, "I have learned for myself that God is good and that His ways are better than mine."

I bear witness of God, our Eternal Father, who loves us; of His Son, Jesus Christ, who saved us. They know our hurts and challenges. They will never forsake us and know perfectly how to succor us. We can be of good cheer as we trust Them more than anyone or anything else. In the sacred name of Jesus Christ, amen.

Notes

1. Louisa Barnes Pratt, in Saints: The Story of the Church of Jesus Christ in the Latter Days, vol. 2, No Unhallowed Hand, 1846–1893 (2020), 103; see also Saints, vol. 1, The Standard of Truth, 1815–1846 (2018), 494–95.
2. After all, He is our Father. He loves us. And, as Elder Patrick Kearon taught, "[He] is in relentless pursuit of [us]. He 'wants all of His children to choose to return to Him' [General Handbook: Serving in The Church of Jesus Christ of Latter-day Saints, 1.1, Gospel Library], and He employs every possible measure to bring [us] back" ("God's Intent Is to Bring You Home," Liahona, May 2024, 87).
3. See 2 Nephi 4:34.
4. See Moses 4:3.
5. See Jacob 7:7; Alma 1:4; 30:13–18, 23–28.
6. See Russell M. Nelson, "Think Celestial!," Liahona, Nov. 2023, 117–19; "The Love and Laws of God" (Brigham Young University devotional, Sept. 17, 2019), speeches.byu.edu; "Pure Truth, Pure Doctrine, and Pure Revelation," Liahona, Nov. 2021, 6–7.
7. Mosiah 4:9.
8. Neil L. Andersen, "The Prophet of God," Ensign or Liahona, May 2018, 26.
9. See Alma 12:9–11.
10. See Alma 32:38–39.
11. John 6:66; see also verse 60.
12. Doctrine and Covenants 6:36.
13. Dieter F. Uchtdorf, "Come, Join with Us," Ensign or Liahona, Nov. 2013, 23.
14. John 6:67–69.
15. Mark 9:23.
16. Mark 9:24.
17. Neal A. Maxwell, "Swallowed Up in the Will of the Father," Ensign, Nov. 1995, 24.
18. Mosiah 3:19.
19. See Doctrine and Covenants 19:18–19.
20. See Acts 5:32; Galatians 3:2; Jarom 1:4; Alma 32:28; Mormon 9:25; Ether 4:11.

GOD LOVES ALL HIS CHILDREN

ELDER GREGORIO E. CASILLAS

Of the Seventy

What does our Heavenly Father desire from you? Do you understand that when you were in your premortal existence, Heavenly Father was preparing you for your life on earth? Speaking to youth, President Russell M. Nelson taught, "Our Heavenly Father has reserved many of His most noble spirits—perhaps . . . His finest team—for this final phase."[1] Because we have been reserved for these latter days, it is crucial for us to learn to be disciples of Jesus Christ.

The Lord Jesus Christ is the Good Shepherd, and He knows His flock, and the flock knows its Shepherd because "he calleth his own sheep by name."[2] He is always calling upon us, and He uses us, His ordinary servants, to help bring His children to Him.

A while ago, a stake president and I were visiting members of the Church in a local neighborhood. After we finished our scheduled visits, the stake president asked me if we could go see one more family. He felt impressed that we should talk with them.

We knocked on the door, and a sister opened it. She looked at me, but she didn't know who I was, so she didn't express much. I pointed my hand toward the stake president, who greeted her by name. As soon as she heard and saw him, she rejoiced. Standing there at the door, they both hugged each other and cried together. This set the tone for our visit. We didn't know that the sister had received chemotherapy the day before. She felt too weak to care for her adult son. So I helped the stake president dress her son, and we put him in his wheelchair. We fed him the food that another sweet sister from the ward had brought earlier, and we helped with other tasks. Before we left their home, we were able to bless them.

All that was going through my mind during this visit was a confirmation that Jesus Christ loves them deeply. He understands them and personally knows the pain of their unique situation. Almost the entire visit happened in silence. On this occasion we did not give a big sermon or share our favorite scripture, but the Lord blessed us with His Spirit abundantly.

One of the greatest reasons your Heavenly Father sent you here at this time is so that you can realize your full potential. *Preach My Gospel* teaches us that as disciples of Christ, we should avoid comparing ourselves to one another.[3] Your spiritual abilities are unique, personal, and innate, and your Heavenly Father wants to help you develop them. There will always be someone you can help feel the love of your Heavenly Father. Your potential is divine. While it's certainly important to prepare yourself to succeed in this very competitive world, one of your crucial missions throughout your life is to become a disciple of Jesus Christ and to follow the impressions of the Spirit. As you do this, God will bless your life; He will bless your current or future family; and He will bless the lives of His children who you encounter.

We live in a time of great opportunity. Although we face many difficulties, I know they are there in part to allow us to help others feel the love of our Heavenly Father. President Nelson taught, "In coming days, we will see the *greatest* manifestations of the Savior's power that the world has *ever* seen."[4] We have the privilege to watch over people who need a helping hand, an embrace, a feeling of comfort, or for us simply to be with them in silence. If we can help lighten their burdens, even if only for a moment, then we will be able to see the great manifestations of the Savior's power in their lives.

As disciples of Jesus Christ, Latter-day Saints can make a positive difference in the world. We can provide a sense of joy that is reflected in our countenance—a joy that we share with words of love and acts of kindness. Let us be good neighbors, good employers, good workers. Let us strive to be good Christians at all times.

The Lord has restored His gospel with the necessary ordinances so that Heavenly Father's children can have all the promises that bind us to Him. By helping our sisters and brothers in their daily challenges, let us also remember to help them make and keep these sacred promises with their Heavenly Father so that He in turn can promise them the richest blessings for this life and for eternity. These promises are only made possible through the Restoration of the gospel of Jesus Christ and His priesthood keys.

In other words, we can help others stay on the covenant path. Some of us deviate from the path from time to time, and so we must remember that for our Heavenly Father we always have the possibility of returning. Even if our course is not the most perfect, the Savior always reminds us, "As oft as [we repent] and [seek] forgiveness, with real intent, [we will be] forgiven."[5]

One of the crafts of the adversary today is to make us think and believe that there is no way for us to change or that we no longer have hope. This destructive thinking causes many of us to stop trying. And it is at this moment when our love, our words of encouragement and support, our time, and our help can give someone hope enough to try once more.

Maybe you are thinking, "OK, but who ministers to me?" By going and blessing the lives of our brothers and sisters, we will collect testimonies that will fill our lives with faith in the Lord Jesus Christ. These testimonies will revitalize us to try once more ourselves. The Holy Spirit will revive us and help us with renewed testimonies to continue with our own difficulties and personal trials. Whenever we seek to bless the lives of others, the Lord takes mercy upon us even more; He strengthens us and helps us in our lives.

Please remember that the Lord Jesus Christ is your Savior and understands you personally. He knows what it is to have to fulfill a calling and leave things behind to help the children of God. He has the power to bless you in everything if you believe in Him and do not doubt.[6]

My dear brothers and sisters, on that day when a priesthood leader felt impressed for us to visit a mother and a son that we did not have on our agenda, I proclaim that God knew they needed us. And at the end, I was the one who was ministered to. On that day, I received one of the greatest lessons of the Savior's love for us.

I testify that Jesus Christ is the Savior of the world, that He lives, that He lived and died for you and me, and that He was resurrected for you and me so that we can aspire to celestial reunions full of joy with those who are already on the other side of the veil. I know that He understands you and me perfectly. He understands each of our difficult moments, and He has the power to help us in those moments when we feel most vulnerable. I know that the Lord Jesus Christ and our Heavenly Father appeared to Joseph Smith to restore the gospel in these days. I know that our dear prophet, President Russell M. Nelson, is a prophet of the Lord, and I testify of these things in the name of Jesus Christ, amen.

Notes

1. Russell M. Nelson, "Hope of Israel" (worldwide youth devotional, June 3, 2018), Gospel Library.
2. See John 10:2–4.
3. "Avoid comparing yourself to other missionaries and measuring the outward results of your efforts with theirs" (*Preach My Gospel: A Guide to Sharing the Gospel of Jesus Christ* [2023], 13).
4. Russell M. Nelson, "Overcome the World and Find Rest," *Liahona*, Nov. 2022, 95.
5. Moroni 6:8.
6. See Alma 56:47; 57:26.

FOLLOWING CHRIST

PRESIDENT DALLIN H. OAKS
First Counselor in the First Presidency

This year millions have been inspired by the gospel study plan known by the Savior's invitation "Come, follow me."[1] Following Christ is not a casual or occasional practice. It is a continuous commitment and way of life that should guide us at all times and in all places. His teachings and His example define the path for every disciple of Jesus Christ. And all are invited to this path, for He invites all to come unto Him, "black and white, bond and free, male and female; . . . and all are alike unto God."[2]

I.

The first step in following Christ is to obey what He defined as "the great commandment in the law":

"Thou shalt love the Lord thy God with all thy heart, and with all thy soul, and with all thy mind.

"This is the first and great commandment.

"And the second is like unto it, Thou shalt love thy neighbour as thyself.

"On these two commandments hang all the law and the prophets."[3]

The commandments of God provide the guiding and steadying force in our lives. Our experiences in mortality are like the little boy and his father flying a kite on a windy day. As the kite rose higher, the winds caused it to tug on the connecting string in the little boy's hand. Inexperienced with the force of mortal winds, he proposed to cut the string so the kite could rise higher. His wise father counseled no, explaining that the string is what holds the kite in place against mortal winds. If we lose our hold on the string, the kite will not rise higher. It will be carried about by these winds and inevitably crash to the earth.

That essential string represents the covenants that connect us to God, our Heavenly Father, and His Son, Jesus Christ. As we honor those covenants by keeping Their commandments and following Their plan of redemption, Their promised blessings enable us to soar to celestial heights.

The Book of Mormon frequently declares that Christ is "the light of the world."[4] During His appearance to the Nephites, the risen Lord explained that teaching by telling them: "I have set an example for you."[5] "I am the light which ye shall hold up—that which ye have seen me do."[6] He is our role model. We learn what He has said and done by studying the scriptures and following prophetic teachings, as President Russell M. Nelson has urged us to do.[7] In the ordinance of the sacrament, we covenant each Sabbath day that we will "always remember him and keep his commandments."[8]

II.

In the Book of Mormon, the Lord gave us the fundamentals in what He called "the doctrine of Christ." These are faith in the Lord Jesus Christ, repentance, baptism, receiving the gift of the Holy Ghost, enduring to the end, and becoming as a little child,[9] which means to trust the Lord and submit to all He requires of us.[10]

The Lord's commandments are of two types: permanent, like the doctrine of Christ, and temporary. Temporary commandments are those necessary for the needs of the Lord's Church or the faithful in temporary circumstances, but to be set aside when the need has passed. An example of temporary commandments are the Lord's directions to the early leadership of the Church to move the Saints from New York to Ohio, to Missouri, and to Illinois and finally to lead the pioneer exodus to the Intermountain West. Though only temporary, when still in force these commandments were given to be obeyed.

Some permanent commandments have taken considerable time to be generally observed. For example, President Lorenzo Snow's famous sermon on the law of tithing emphasized a commandment given earlier but not yet generally observed by Church members.[11] It needed reemphasis in the circumstances then faced by the Church and its members. Recent examples of reemphases have also been needed because of current circumstances faced by Latter-day Saints or the Church. These include the proclamation on the family, issued by President Gordon B. Hinckley a generation ago,[12] and President Russell M. Nelson's recent call for the Church to be known by its revealed name, The Church of Jesus Christ of Latter-day Saints.[13]

III.

Another of our Savior's teachings seems to require reemphasis in the circumstances of our day.

This is a time of many harsh and hurtful words in public communications and sometimes even in our families. Sharp differences on issues of public policy often result in actions of hostility—even hatred—in public and personal relationships. This atmosphere of enmity sometimes even paralyzes capacities for lawmaking on matters of importance where most citizens see an urgent need for some action in the public interest.

What should followers of Christ teach and do in this time of toxic communications? What were His teachings and examples?

It is significant that among the first principles Jesus taught when He appeared to the Nephites was to avoid contention. While He taught this in the context of disputes over religious doctrine, the reasons He gave clearly apply to communications and relationships in politics, public policy, and family relationships. Jesus taught:

"He that hath the spirit of contention is not of me, but is of the devil, who is the father of contention, and he stirreth up the hearts of men to contend with anger, one with another.

"Behold, this is not my doctrine, to stir up the hearts of men with anger, one against another; but this is my doctrine, that such things should be done away."[14]

In His remaining ministry among the Nephites, Jesus taught other commandments closely related to His prohibition of contention. We know from the Bible that He had previously taught each of these in His great Sermon on the Mount, usually in precisely the same language He later used with the Nephites. I will quote the familiar Bible language:

"Love your enemies, bless them that curse you, do good to them that hate you, and pray for them which despitefully use you, and persecute you."[15]

This is one of Christ's best-known commandments—most revolutionary and most difficult to follow. Yet it is a most fundamental part of His invitation for all to follow Him. As President David O. McKay taught, "There is no better way to manifest love for God than to show an unselfish love for one's fellowmen."[16]

Here is another fundamental teaching by Him who is our role model: "Blessed are the peacemakers: for they shall be called the children of God."[17]

Peacemakers! How it would change personal relationships if followers of Christ would forgo harsh and hurtful words in all their communications.

In general conference last year, President Russell M. Nelson gave us these challenges:

"One of the easiest ways to identify a *true follower* of Jesus Christ is how compassionately that person treats other people. . . .

" . . . True disciples of Jesus Christ are peacemakers.

" . . . One of the best ways we can honor the Savior is to become a peacemaker."

Concluding his teachings: "Contention is a choice. Peacemaking is a choice. You have your agency to choose contention or reconciliation. I urge you to *choose* to be a peacemaker, now and always."[18]

Potential adversaries should begin their discussions by identifying common ground on which all agree.

To follow our Perfect Role Model and His prophet, we need to practice what is popularly known as the Golden Rule: "All things whatsoever ye would that men should do to you, do ye even so to them: for this is the law and the prophets."[19] We need to love and do good to all. We need to avoid contention and be peacemakers in all our communications. This does not mean to compromise our principles and priorities but to cease harshly attacking others for theirs. That is what our Perfect Role Model did in His ministry. That is the example He set for us as He invited us to follow Him.

In this conference four years ago, President Nelson gave us a prophetic challenge for our own day:

"Are *you* willing to let God prevail in your life? Are *you* willing to let God be the most important influence in your life? Will you allow His words, His commandments, and His covenants to influence what you do each day? Will you allow His voice to take priority over any other?"[20]

As followers of Christ, we teach and testify of Jesus Christ, our Perfect Role Model. So let us follow Him by forgoing contention. As we pursue our preferred policies in public actions, let us qualify for His blessings by using the language and methods of peacemakers. In our families and other personal relationships, let us avoid what is harsh and hateful. Let us seek to be holy, like our Savior, in whose holy name I testify and invoke His blessing to help us be Saints. In the name of Jesus Christ, amen.

Notes

1. Luke 18:22.
2. 2 Nephi 26:33.
3. Matthew 22:36–40.
4. Alma 38:9; see also Mosiah 16:9; 3 Nephi 9:18.
5. 3 Nephi 18:16.
6. 3 Nephi 18:24; see also 3 Nephi 27:21.
7. See Russell M. Nelson, "Drawing the Power of Jesus Christ into Our Lives," *Ensign* or *Liahona*, May 2017, 39–40.
8. Doctrine and Covenants 20:77.
9. See 3 Nephi 11:32–33, 38; see also 2 Nephi 31:13–21; 3 Nephi 27:13–22.
10. See Mosiah 3:19.
11. See *Saints: The Story of the Church of Jesus Christ in the Latter Days*, vol. 3, *Boldly, Nobly, and Independent, 1893–1955* (2022), 73–77.
12. See "The Family: A Proclamation to the World," Gospel Library.
13. See Russell M. Nelson, "The Correct Name of the Church," *Ensign* or *Liahona*, Nov. 2018, 87–89.
14. 3 Nephi 11:29–30.
15. Matthew 5:44; see also 3 Nephi 12:44.
16. *Teachings of Presidents of the Church: David O. McKay* (2003), 181.
17. Matthew 5:9; see also 3 Nephi 12:9.
18. Russell M. Nelson, "Peacemakers Needed," *Liahona*, May 2023, 98, 99, 100.
19. Matthew 7:12.
20. Russell M. Nelson, "Let God Prevail," *Ensign* or *Liahona*, Nov. 2020, 94.

Saturday Afternoon Session

OCTOBER 5, 2024

BURYING OUR WEAPONS OF REBELLION

ELDER D. TODD CHRISTOFFERSON

Of the Quorum of the Twelve Apostles

The Book of Mormon records that approximately 90 years before the birth of Christ, the sons of King Mosiah began what would be a 14-year mission to the Lamanites. Unsuccessful efforts had been made over many generations to bring the Lamanite people to a belief in the doctrine of Christ.[1] This time, however, through the miraculous interventions of the Holy Spirit, thousands of the Lamanites were converted and became disciples of Jesus Christ.

We read, "And as sure as the Lord liveth, so sure as many as believed, or as many as were brought to the knowledge of the truth, through the preaching of Ammon and his brethren, according to the spirit of revelation and of prophecy, and the power of God working miracles in them—yea, I say unto you, as the Lord liveth, as many of the Lamanites as believed in their preaching, and were converted unto the Lord, never did fall away."[2]

The key to the enduring conversion of this people is stated in the next verse: "For they became a righteous people; they did lay down the weapons of their rebellion, that they did not fight against God any more, neither against any of their brethren."[3]

This reference to "weapons of rebellion" was both literal and figurative. It meant their swords and other weapons of war but also their disobedience to God and His commandments.

The king of these converted Lamanites expressed it this way: "And now behold, my brethren, . . . it has been all that we could do . . . to repent of all our sins and the many murders which we have committed, and to get God *to take them away from our hearts*, for it was all we could do to repent sufficiently before God that he would *take away our stain*."[4]

Note the king's words—not only had their sincere repentance led to forgiveness of their sins, but God also took away the stain of those sins and even the desire to sin from their hearts. As you know, rather than risk any possible return to their prior state of rebellion against God, they buried their swords. And as they buried their physical weapons, with changed hearts, they also buried their disposition to sin.

We might ask ourselves what we could do to follow this pattern, to "lay down the weapons of [our] rebellion," whatever they may be, and become so "converted [to] the Lord" that the stain of sin and the desire for sin are taken from our hearts and we never will fall away.

Rebellion can be active or passive. The classic example of willful rebellion is Lucifer, who, in the premortal world, opposed the Father's plan of redemption and rallied others to oppose it as well, "and, at that day, many followed after him."[5] It is not hard to discern the impact of his continuing rebellion in our own time.

The Book of Mormon's unholy trio of anti-Christs—Sherem, Nehor, and Korihor—provide a classic study of active rebellion against God. The overarching thesis of Nehor and Korihor was that there is no sin; therefore, there is no need for repentance, and there is no Savior. "Every man prosper[s] according to his genius, and . . . every man conquer[s] according to his strength; and whatsoever a man [does is] no crime."[6] The anti-Christ rejects religious authority, characterizing ordinances and covenants as performances "laid down by ancient priests, to usurp power and authority."[7]

A latter-day example of willful rebellion with a happier ending is the story of William W. Phelps. Phelps joined the Church in 1831 and was appointed Church printer. He edited several early Church publications, wrote numerous hymns, and served as a scribe to Joseph Smith. Unfortunately, he turned against the Church and the Prophet, even to the point of giving false testimony against Joseph Smith in a Missouri court, which contributed to the Prophet's imprisonment there.

Later, Phelps wrote to Joseph asking for forgiveness. "I know my situation, you know it, and God knows it, and I want to be saved if my friends will help me."

In his reply the Prophet stated: "It is true that we have suffered much in consequence of your behavior. . . . However, the cup has been drunk, the will of our Heavenly Father has been done, and we are yet alive. . . . Come on, dear brother, since the war is past, for friends at first are friends again at last."[8]

With sincere repentance, William Phelps buried his "weapons of rebellion" and was received once more in full fellowship, never again to fall away.

Perhaps the more insidious form of rebellion against God, however, is the passive version—ignoring His will in our lives. Many who would never consider active rebellion may still oppose the will and word of God by pursuing their own path without regard to divine direction. I am reminded of the song made famous years ago by singer Frank Sinatra with the climactic line "I did it my way." Certainly in life there is plenty of room for personal preference and individual choice, but when it comes to matters of salvation and eternal life, our theme song ought to be "I did it God's way," because truly there is no other way.

Take, for instance, the Savior's example regarding baptism. He submitted to baptism as a demonstration of loyalty to the Father and as an example to us:

"He showeth unto the children of men that, according to the flesh he humbleth himself before the Father, and witnesseth unto the Father that he would be obedient unto him in keeping his commandments. . . .

"And he said unto the children of men: Follow thou me. Wherefore, my beloved brethren, can we follow Jesus save we shall be willing to keep the commandments of the Father?"[9]

There is no "my way" if we are to follow Christ's example. Trying to find a different course to heaven is like the futility of working on the Tower of Babel rather than looking to Christ and His salvation.

The swords and other weapons that the Lamanite converts buried were weapons of rebellion because of how they had used them. Those same kinds of weapons in the hands of their sons, being used in defense of family and freedom, were not weapons of rebellion against God at all.[10] The same was true of such weapons in the hands of the Nephites: "They were not fighting for monarchy nor power but . . . were fighting for their homes and their liberties, their wives and their children, and their all, yea, for their rites of worship and their church."[11]

In this same way, there are things in our lives that may be neutral or even inherently good but that used in the wrong way become "weapons of rebellion." Our speech, for example, can edify or demean. As James said:

"But the tongue [it seems] can no man tame; it is an unruly evil, full of deadly poison.

"Therewith bless we God, even the Father; and therewith curse we men, which are made after the similitude of God.

"Out of the same mouth proceedeth blessing and cursing. My brethren, these things ought not so to be."[12]

There is much in public and personal discourse today that is malicious and mean-spirited. There is much conversation that is vulgar and profane, even among youth. This sort of speech is a "weapon of rebellion" against God, "full of deadly poison."[13]

Consider another example of something that is essentially good but that could be turned against divine directives—a person's career. One can find real satisfaction in a profession, vocation, or service, and all of us are benefited by what devoted and talented people in many fields of endeavor have accomplished and created.

Still, it is possible that devotion to career can become the paramount focus of one's life. Then all else becomes secondary, including any claim the Savior may make on one's time and talent. For men, and for women as well, forgoing legitimate opportunities for marriage, failing to cleave to and lift one's spouse, failing to nurture one's children, or even intentionally avoiding the blessing and responsibility of child-rearing solely for the sake of career advancement can convert laudable achievement into a form of rebellion.

Another example concerns our physical being. Paul reminds us that we are to glorify God in both body and spirit[14] and that this body is the temple of the Holy Ghost, "which ye have of God, and ye are not your own."[15] Thus, we have a legitimate interest in spending time caring for our bodies as best we can. Few of us will reach the peak of performance we have seen recently in the achievements of Olympic and Paralympic athletes, and some of us are experiencing the effects of age, or what President M. Russell Ballard called "the rivets coming loose."

Nevertheless, I believe it pleases our Creator when we do our best to care for His wonderful gift of a physical body. It would be a mark of rebellion to deface or defile one's body, or abuse it, or fail to do what one can to pursue a healthy lifestyle. At the same time, vanity and becoming consumed with one's physique, appearance, or dress can be a form of rebellion at the other extreme, leading one to worship God's gift instead of God.

In the end, burying our weapons of rebellion against God simply means yielding to the enticing of the Holy Spirit, putting off the natural man, and becoming "a saint through the atonement of Christ the Lord."[16] It means putting the first commandment first in our lives. It means letting God prevail. If our love of God and our determination to serve Him with all our might, mind, and strength become the touchstone by which we judge all things and make all our decisions, we will have buried our weapons of rebellion. By the grace of Christ, God will forgive our sins and rebellions of the past and will take away the stain of those sins and rebellions from our hearts. In time, He will even take away any desire for evil, as He did with those Lamanite converts of the past. Thereafter, we too "never [will] fall away."[17]

Burying our weapons of rebellion leads to a unique joy. With all who have ever become converted to the Lord, we are "brought to sing [the song of] redeeming love."[18] Our Heavenly Father and His Son, our Redeemer, have confirmed Their unending commitment to our ultimate happiness through the most profound love and sacrifice. We experience Their love daily. Surely we can reciprocate with our own love and loyalty. May we bury—very, very deep—any element of rebellion against God in our lives and replace it with a willing heart and a willing mind.[19] In the name of Jesus Christ, amen.

Notes

1. See, for example, Jacob 7:24; Enos 1:14, 20.
2. Alma 23:6.
3. Alma 23:7.
4. Alma 24:11; emphasis added.
5. Abraham 3:28; see also Revelation 12:7–9.
6. Alma 30:17.
7. Alma 30:23; see also verses 27–28.
8. *Saints: The Story of the Church of Jesus Christ in the Latter Days*, vol. 1, *The Standard of Truth, 1815–1846* (2018), 418; see also "Letter from William W. Phelps, with Appended Letter from Orson Hyde and John E. Page, 29 June 1840" and Joseph Smith, "Letter to William W. Phelps, 22 July 1840," josephsmithpapers.org.
9. 2 Nephi 31:7, 10.
10. See Alma 53:17–18.
11. Alma 43:45; see also verse 47; Alma 48:14–16.
12. James 3:8–10.
13. James 3:8. "Make sure your language reflects love of God and others—whether you're communicating in person or virtually. Say things that uplift—nothing that might be divisive, hurtful, or offensive, even as a joke. Your words can be powerful. Let them be powerful for good" (*For the Strength of Youth: A Guide for Making Choices* [2022], 12).
14. See 1 Corinthians 6:20.
15. 1 Corinthians 6:19.
16. Mosiah 3:19.
17. Alma 23:6.
18. Alma 26:13.
19. See Doctrine and Covenants 64:34.

BONDED TO JESUS CHRIST: BECOMING THE SALT OF THE EARTH

ELDER JOSÉ A. TEIXEIRA

Of the Presidency of the Seventy

The Savior taught that when we are "called unto [His] everlasting gospel, and covenant with an everlasting covenant, [we] are accounted as the salt of the earth."[1] Salt is made of two elements bonded together. We can't be salt on our own; if we are to be salt of the earth, we must be bonded to the Lord, and that is what I see as I mingle with members of the Church around the world—I see faithful members of the Church bonded to the Lord, committed in their efforts to serve others and be the salt of the earth.

Your unwavering dedication is a shining example. Your service is appreciated and cherished.

Our youth have shown remarkable courage and devotion. They have enthusiastically embraced the work of family history, and their frequent visits to the house of the Lord are a testament to their dedication. Their willingness to devote time and energy to serve missions across the globe reflects a deep and abiding faith. They are not merely participating but leading the way in becoming disciples bonded to Jesus Christ. Their service radiates light and hope, touching countless lives. To you, the youth of the Church, we express our heartfelt thanks for your inspiring service. You are not just the Church's future but its present. And you are indeed the salt of the earth!

I love the Lord Jesus Christ and feel blessed by the opportunity to serve alongside you in the Lord's Church. Our unity and strength, grounded in our shared faith, reassure us that we are never alone in this journey. Together, we can continue to build the kingdom of God, rooted in service, love, and unwavering faith.

When Jesus Christ taught by the Sea of Galilee, He often used everyday elements familiar to His audience to convey profound spiritual truths. One such element was salt. Jesus declared, "[You] are the salt of the earth,"[2] a statement rich in meaning and significance, especially for the people of His time, who understood the multi-faceted value of salt.

The ancient craft of salt harvesting in the Algarve, the southern region of my home country of Portugal, dates back thousands of years to the era of the Roman Empire. Remarkably, the methods used by the salt workers, known as *marnotos*, have changed little since then. These dedicated artisans employ traditional techniques, performing their work entirely by hand, maintaining a legacy that has endured through the centuries.

This ancient method harvests what is called "flower of salt." To fully appreciate the intricate process of harvesting the flower of salt, it is essential to understand the environment in which it is produced. The Algarve's coastal salt marshes provide the ideal conditions for salt production. Seawater is channeled into shallow ponds, known as salt pans, where it is left to evaporate under the intense sun. As the water evaporates, the flower of salt forms delicate crystals on the surface of the salt pans. These crystals are incredibly pure and have a unique, crisp texture. The *marnotos* carefully skim the crystals from the water's surface using specialized tools, a process that requires great skill and precision. In Portugal, this fine-quality salt is referred to as "salt cream" because it can be gently skimmed away like cream rising to the top of milk. This delicate salt is cherished for its purity and exceptional flavor, making it a prized ingredient in culinary arts.

Just like the *marnotos* put forth great effort to ensure they harvest the highest quality of salt, so should we, as the Lord's covenant people, always do our very best so that our love and example are, as much as possible, a pure reflection of our Savior, Jesus Christ.

In the ancient world, salt was more than just a seasoning—it was a vital preservative and a symbol of purity and covenant. People knew that salt was essential for preserving food and enhancing flavor. They also understood the grave implications of salt losing its saltiness, or savor, by becoming contaminated or diluted.

Like salt can lose its essence, we can also lose our spiritual vitality if our faith in Jesus Christ becomes casual. We may look the same on the outside, but without a strong inner faith, we lose our ability to make a difference in the world and bring out the best in those around us.

So how can we channel our energy and efforts to make a difference and be the change the world needs today? How can we preserve discipleship and continue to be a positive influence?

The words of our dear prophet still echo in my mind: "God wants us to work together and help each other. That is why He sends us to earth in families and organizes us into wards and stakes. That is why He asks us to serve and minister to each other. That is why He asks us to live *in* the world but not be *of* the world."[3]

When our lives are filled with purpose and service, we avoid spiritual apathy; on the other hand, when our lives are deprived of divine purpose, meaningful service to others, and sacred opportunities for pondering and reflection, we gradually become suffocated by our own activity and self-interest, risking losing our savor. The antidote to this is to continue to be involved in service—being anxiously engaged in good works and the betterment of ourselves and the society we live in.

My dear brothers and sisters, what a blessing we all have today to belong to the Church of Jesus Christ and have the opportunity to serve in His Church. Our circumstances may vary, but we all can make a difference.

Remember the *marnotos*, the salt workers; they use simple tools to harvest the best crystals, the best salt! We too can do simple things that, with consistent efforts in small and meaningful acts, can deepen our discipleship and commitment to Jesus Christ. Here are four simple yet profound ways we can strive to be the salt of the earth:

1. Keeping the house of the Lord at the center of our devotion. Now that temples are closer than ever before, prioritizing regular worship in the house of the Lord will help us focus on what matters most and keep our lives centered in Christ. In the temple, we find the heart of our faith in Jesus Christ and the soul of our devotion to Him.

2. Being deliberate in our efforts to strengthen others by living

the gospel together. We can strengthen our families through consistent and intentional efforts to bring gospel principles into our lives and to our homes.

3. Being willing to accept a calling and serving in the Church. Service in our local congregations allows us to support one another and grow together. While serving is not always convenient, it is always rewarding.

4. And finally, using digital communication tools with purpose. Today, digital communication tools allow us to connect as never before. Like most of you, I use these tools to connect with brothers and sisters in the Church and with my family and friends. As I connect with them, I feel closer to them; we can minister to each other in times of need when we cannot be physically present. These tools are undoubtedly a blessing, yet these very same tools can drag us away from the depth of meaningful interactions and eventually cause us to be pulled into habits that waste our time in less purposeful activities. Striving to be the salt of the earth includes so much more than an endless scrolling of reels on a six-inch screen.

As we keep the house of the Lord central in our lives, intentionally strengthen others by living the gospel, accept callings to serve, and use digital tools with purpose, we can preserve our spiritual vitality. Just as salt in its purest form has the power to enhance and preserve, so too does our faith in Jesus Christ when it is nourished and protected by our dedication to Christlike service and love.

As we remain bonded to the Lord, our lives will naturally reflect His light, and we will become the salt of the earth. In this effort, we not only enrich our lives but also strengthen our families and our communities. May we strive to maintain this bond with the Lord, never lose our savor, and be the small, little crystal of salt that the Lord wants us to be. In the name of Jesus Christ, amen.

Notes

1. Doctrine and Covenants 101:39.
2. Matthew 5:13.
3. Russell M. Nelson, "What We Are Learning and Will Never Forget," *Liahona*, May 2021, 79.

HIS HAND READY TO HELP US

ELDER JUAN PABLO VILLAR
Of the Seventy

When I was a child, as a family we went on vacation to a beach on the coast of my native country, Chile. I was excited to spend some days enjoying the summer with my family. I was also thrilled because I thought I could finally join in and do what my two older brothers usually did for fun on the water.

One day my brothers went to play where the waves were breaking, and I felt big and mature enough to follow them. As I moved toward that area, I realized the waves were larger than they appeared from the shore. Suddenly, a wave rapidly approached me, taking me by surprise. I felt like the power of nature had taken over me, and I was dragged into the depths of the sea. I couldn't see or feel any reference point as I was tossed around. Just as I thought my adventure on the earth might be coming to an end, I felt a hand pulling me toward the surface. Finally, I could see the sun and catch my breath.

My brother Claudio had seen my attempts to act as a grown-up and had come to my rescue. I was not far from the shore. Even though the water was shallow, I was disoriented and had not realized I could have helped myself. Claudio told me that I needed to be careful and, if I wanted, he could teach me. Despite the gallons of water I had swallowed, my pride and desire to be a big boy were stronger, and I said, "Sure."

Claudio told me I needed to attack the waves. I told myself I would surely lose that battle against what seemed like a huge wall of water.

As a new big wave approached, Claudio quickly said, "Look at me; this is how you do it." Claudio ran toward the incoming wave and dove into it before it broke. I was so impressed with his dive that I lost sight of the next incoming wave. So again I was sent to the depths of the sea and tossed by the forces of nature. A few seconds later, a hand grasped mine, and I was again pulled toward the surface and air. The flame of my pride was extinguishing.

This time my brother invited me to dive with him. As per his invitation, I followed him, and we dove together. I felt as if I was conquering the most complicated challenge. Certainly, it was not very easy, but I did it, thanks to the help and example shown by my brother. His hand rescued me twice; his example showed me how to deal with my challenge and be victorious that day.

President Russell M. Nelson has invited us to think celestial,[1] and I want to follow his advice and apply it to my summer story.

The Savior's Power over the Adversary

If we think celestial, we will understand that in our lives we will face challenges that seem greater than our capacity to overcome them. During our mortal time, we are subject to the attacks of the adversary. Like the waves that had power over me that summer day, we can feel powerless and want to give in to a stronger fate. Those "malicious waves" could jostle us from side to side. But do not forget who has power over those waves and, in fact, over all things.[2] That is our Savior, Jesus Christ. He has the power to help us out of every miserable condition or adverse situation. Regardless of whether we feel close to Him, He still can reach us where we are as we are.

As we reach out to Him in faith, He will always be there, and in His time, He will be ready and willing to grasp our hands and pull us up to a safe place.[3]

The Savior and His Ministering Example

If we think celestial, we will recognize Jesus Christ as a flawless example of ministry. There is a pattern for us in the scriptures when He or His disciples reach out to someone in need of help, rescue, or a blessing as they reach out with their hands. As in my story, I knew my brother was there, but being there for me was not enough. Claudio knew I was in trouble, and he went to help lift me from the water.

Occasionally, we think that we only need to be there for someone in need, and many times there is more we can do. Having an eternal perspective can help us receive revelation to offer timely assistance to others in need. We can rely on the guidance and inspiration of the Holy Ghost to discern what kind of help is needed, whether it is temporal support like emotional comfort, food, or aid with daily tasks, or spiritual guidance to help others in their journey to prepare, make, and honor sacred covenants.[5]

The Savior Is Ready to Rescue Us

When Peter, the senior Apostle, "walked on the water, to go to Jesus, . . . he was afraid; and beginning to sink"; then "he cried, saying, Lord, save me." Jesus knew the faith Peter had exercised to come unto Him on the water. He was also aware of Peter's fear. According to the account, Jesus "immediately . . . stretched forth his hand, and caught him," saying the following words: "O thou of little faith, wherefore didst thou doubt?"[7] His words were not to scold Peter but to remind him that He, the Messiah, was with him and the disciples.

If we think celestial, we will receive the confirmation in our hearts that Jesus Christ is indeed our Rescuer, our Advocate with the Father, and our Redeemer. As we exercise faith in Him, He will save us from our fallen state, beyond our challenges, infirmities, and needs in this temporal life, and give us the greatest of all gifts, which is eternal life.

The Savior Does Not Give Up on Us

My brother did not give up on me that day but persisted so I could learn how to do it for myself. He persisted, even if that required rescuing me *twice*. He persisted, even if I could not get it at first. He persisted so I could overcome that challenge and succeed. If we think celestial, we will realize that our Savior will be there as many times as necessary to provide help if we want to learn, change, overcome, cope, or succeed in whatever will bring true and everlasting happiness to our lives.[8]

The Savior's Hands

The scriptures immortalize the symbol and significance of the Savior's hands. In His atoning sacrifice, His hands were pierced by nails to affix Him to the cross. After His Resurrection, He appeared to His disciples in a perfect body, but the prints in His hands remain as a reminder of His infinite sacrifice.[9] His hand will always be there for us, even if we cannot see it or feel it at first, because He was chosen by our Heavenly Father to be our Savior, the Redeemer of all humankind.

If I think celestial, I know that we are not left alone in this life. While we must face challenges and trials, our Heavenly Father knows our capabilities and knows we can bear or overcome our difficulties. We must do our part and turn to Him in faith. His Beloved Son, Jesus Christ, is our rescuer and will always be there. In His name, the sacred name of Jesus Christ, amen.

Notes

1. See Russell M. Nelson, "Think Celestial!," *Liahona*, Nov. 2023, 118:
   "When you make choices, I invite you to take the long view—an eternal view. Put Jesus Christ first because your eternal life is dependent upon your faith in Him and in His Atonement. . . .
   "When you are confronted with a dilemma, think celestial! When tested by temptation, think celestial! When life or loved ones let you down, think celestial! When someone dies prematurely, think celestial. When someone lingers with a devastating illness, think celestial. When the pressures of life crowd in upon you, think celestial! As you recover from an accident or injury, as I am doing now, think celestial!"
2. See Mark 4:35–41.
3. While we believe that our Heavenly Father and Jesus Christ have the ability to help us whenever we need it, Their help may not always come in the way we expect. It's important to trust that They know us better than we know ourselves and will provide the support and assistance that is best for us at the right time: "Know thou, my son, that all these things shall give thee experience, and shall be for thy good" (Doctrine and Covenants 122:7).
   The trials and challenges we face help us develop the strength and character to resist temptation and overcome the natural man.
4. See Matthew 14:31; Mark 1:31; 5:41; 9:27; Acts 3:7; 3 Nephi 18:36.
5. When President Russell M. Nelson invited us to minister in a newer and holier way (see "Ministering," *Ensign* or *Liahona*, May 2018, 100), he also asked us to understand that this new way of ministering is not about us and what we want to offer but what others need. Jesus Christ is giving us the opportunity to love our neighbor (see Luke 10:27) in a higher and holier way.
6. Matthew 14:29–30.
7. Matthew 14:31.
8. To truly understand happiness, we need to understand the role of blessings in our lives. The definition of *blessings* helps to clarify this concept: a blessing is "to confer divine favor upon someone. Anything contributing to true happiness, well-being, or prosperity is a blessing" (Guide to the Scriptures, "Bless, Blessed, Blessing," Gospel Library). The world often confuses true happiness with temporary pleasure, which imitates a "happiness" that is short-lived.
9. See Isaiah 49:16.

WELCOME TO THE CHURCH OF JOY

ELDER PATRICK KEARON
Of the Quorum of the Twelve Apostles

I was baptised into The Church of Jesus Christ of Latter-day Saints on Christmas Eve of 1987, nearly 37 years ago. That was a truly wonderful day in my life and in my eternal journey, and I'm profoundly grateful for the friends who prepared the way and brought me to the waters of that new birth.

Whether your baptism was yesterday or years ago, whether you meet in a large multiward Church building or under a thatched canopy, whether you receive the sacrament in remembrance of the Saviour in Thai or Swahili, I would like to say to you, welcome to the church of joy! Welcome to the church of joy!

The Church of Joy

Because of the loving plan of our Heavenly Father for each of His children, and because of the redeeming life and mission of our Saviour, Jesus Christ, we can—and should—be the most joyful people on earth! Even as the storms of life in an often troubled world pound upon us, we can cultivate a growing and abiding sense of joy and inner peace because of our hope in Christ and our understanding of our own place in the beautiful plan of happiness.

The Lord's senior Apostle, President Russell M. Nelson, has spoken of the joy that comes from a life centered on Jesus Christ in nearly every address he has given since becoming the President of the Church. He summed it up so concisely: "Joy comes from and because of Him. . . . For Latter-day Saints, Jesus Christ is joy!"[1]

We are members of the Church of Jesus Christ. We are members of the church of joy! And nowhere should our joy as a people be more apparent than when we gather together each Sabbath in our sacrament meetings to worship the source of all joy! Here we assemble with our ward and branch families to celebrate the sacrament of the Lord's Supper, our deliverance from sin and death, and the Saviour's powerful grace! Here we come to experience the joy, refuge, forgiveness, thanksgiving, and belonging found through Jesus Christ!

Is this spirit of collective rejoicing in Christ what you find? Is this what you bring? Maybe you think this doesn't have much to do with you, or perhaps you are simply used to how things have always been done. But we can all contribute, no matter our age or our calling, to making our sacrament meetings the joy-filled, Christ-focused, welcoming hour they can be, alive with a spirit of joyful reverence.

Joyful Reverence

Joyful reverence? "Is that a thing?" you may ask. Well, yes, it is! We deeply love, honour, and respect our God, and our reverence flows from a soul that rejoices in Christ's abundant love, mercy, and salvation! This joyful reverence to the Lord should characterise our sacred sacrament meetings.

However, for many, reverence only means this: folding our arms tightly around our chests, bowing our heads, closing our eyes, and holding still—indefinitely! This might be a helpful way to teach energetic young children, but as we grow and learn, let us see that reverence is so much more than this. Is that how we would be if the Saviour were with us? No, for "in [His] presence is fulness of joy"![2]

Well, for many of us this transformation in sacrament services will take practice.

Attending versus Worshipping

We do not gather on the Sabbath simply to attend sacrament meeting and check it off the list. We come together to worship. There is a significant difference between the two. To *attend* means to be present at. But to *worship* is to intentionally praise and adore our God in a way that transforms us!

On the Stand and in the Congregation

If we are gathering in remembrance of the Saviour and the redemption He has made possible, our faces should reflect our joy and gratitude! Elder F. Enzio Busche once told the story of when he was a branch president and a young boy in the congregation looked at him on the stand and asked loudly, "What is the man with that mean face doing up there?"[3] Those who sit on the stand—speakers, leaders, choirs—and those who gather in the congregation communicate to each other this "welcome to the church of joy" through the expressions they wear on their faces!

Hymn Singing

As we sing, are we joining together to praise our God and King no matter the quality of our voices, or are we just mumbling or not singing at all? Scripture records that "the song of the righteous is a prayer unto [God]" in which His soul delights.[4] So let's sing! And praise Him![5]

Talks and Testimonies

We center our talks and testimonies on Heavenly Father and Jesus Christ and the fruits of humbly living Their gospel, fruits that are "sweet above all that is sweet." Then we truly "feast . . . even until [we] are filled, that [we] hunger not, neither . . . thirst,"[6] and our burdens become lighter through the joy of the Son.[7]

The Sacrament

The glorious focal point of our services is the blessing and receiving of the sacrament itself, the bread and the water representing the atoning gift of our Lord and the whole purpose of our gathering. This is "a sacred time of spiritual renewal"[8] when we witness anew that we are willing to take upon us the name of Jesus Christ and make again the covenant to always remember the Saviour and keep His commandments.[9]

In some seasons of life, we may approach the sacrament with heavy hearts and overwhelming loads. At other times, we come free and unburdened from cares and troubles. As we listen intently to the blessing of the bread and water[10] and partake of those sacred tokens, we may feel to reflect on the sacrifice of the Saviour, His agonies in Gethsemane, His anguish on the cross, and the sorrows and pains He endured on our behalf. That will be what relieves our souls as we connect our suffering to His. At other times, we will feel to wonder with grateful awe at the "exquisite and sweet" joy of what Jesus's magnificent gift has made possible in our lives and in our eternities![11] We will rejoice for what is yet to come—our cherished reunion with our beloved Father and risen Saviour.

We may have been conditioned to suppose that the purpose of the sacrament is to sit in the pew thinking only about all the ways we messed up during the week before. But let's turn that practice on its head. In the stillness, we can ponder the many ways we have seen the Lord relentlessly pursue us with His wonderful love that week! We can reflect on what it means to "discover the *joy* of daily repentance."[12] We can give thanks for the times the Saviour entered into our struggles and our triumphs and the occasions when we felt His grace, forgiveness, and power giving us strength to overcome our hardships and bear our burdens with patience and even good cheer.[13]

Yes, we ponder the sufferings and injustices inflicted upon our Redeemer for our sin, and that does cause sober reflection. But we sometimes get stuck there—in the garden, at the cross, inside the tomb. We fail to move upward to the joy of the tomb bursting open, the defeat of death, and Christ's victory over all that might prevent us from gaining peace and returning to our heavenly home. Whether we shed tears of sorrow or tears of gratitude during the sacrament, let it be in awesome wonder at the good news of the Father's gift of His Son![14]

Parents with Children Who Are Young or Have Special Needs

Now, for parents of children who are young or have special needs, there is often no such thing as a time of stillness and quiet reflection during the sacrament. But in small moments throughout the week, you can teach by example the love, gratitude, and joy you feel for and from the Saviour as you constantly care for His little lambs. No effort in this pursuit is wasted. God is so aware of you.

Family, Ward, and Branch Councils

Likewise at home, we can begin to enhance our hopes and expectations for our time at church. In family councils, we can discuss how each individual can contribute in meaningful ways to welcoming all to the church of joy! We can plan and expect to have a joyful experience at church.

Ward and branch councils can envision and create a culture of joyful reverence for our sacrament hour, identifying practical steps and visual cues to help.

Joy

Joy looks different for different people. For some, it may be exuberant greetings at the door. For others, it might be quietly helping people feel comfortable by smiling and sitting next to them with a kind and open heart. For those who feel left out or on the margins, the warmth of this welcome will be crucial. Ultimately, we can ask ourselves how the Saviour would want our sacrament hour to be. How would He want each one of His children to be welcomed, cared for, nourished, and loved? How would He want us to feel when we come to be renewed through remembering and worshipping Him?

Conclusion

At the start of my journey of faith, joy in Jesus Christ was my first great discovery, and it changed my world. If you have yet to discover this joy, embark on its quest. This is an invitation to receive the Saviour's gift of peace, light, and joy—to revel in it, to wonder at it, and to rejoice in it every Sabbath.

Ammon in the Book of Mormon expresses the feelings of my heart when he says:

"Now have we not reason to rejoice? Yea, I say unto you, there never were [a people] that had so great reason to rejoice as we, since the world began; yea, and my joy is carried away, even unto boasting in my God; for he has all power, all wisdom, and all understanding; he comprehendeth all things, and he is a merciful Being, even unto salvation, to those who will repent and believe on his name.

"Now if this is boasting, even so will I boast; for this is my life and my light, . . . my joy, and my great thanksgiving."[15]

Welcome to the church of joy! In the name of Jesus Christ, amen.

Notes

1. President Russell M. Nelson taught: "Joy is powerful, and focusing on joy brings God's power into our lives. As in all things, Jesus Christ is our ultimate exemplar, 'who for the joy that was set before him endured the cross' [Hebrews 12:2]. Think of that! In order for Him to endure the most excruciating experience ever endured on earth, our Savior focused on *joy*! And what was the joy that was set before Him? Surely it included the joy of cleansing, healing, and strengthening us; the joy of paying for the sins of all who would repent; the joy of making it possible for you and me to return home—clean and worthy—to live with our Heavenly Parents and families. If we focus on the joy that will come to us, or to those we love, what can we endure that presently seems overwhelming, painful, scary, unfair, or simply impossible?" ("Joy and Spiritual Survival," *Ensign* or *Liahona*, Nov. 2016, 82–83).
2. Psalm 16:11.
3. F. Enzio Busche, "Lessons from the Lamb of God," *Religious Educator*, vol. 9, no. 2 (2008), 3.
4. Doctrine and Covenants 25:12.
5. See Psalm 100:1.
6. Alma 32:42.
7. See Alma 33:23.
8. *General Handbook: Serving in The Church of Jesus Christ of Latter-day Saints*, 29.2.1.1, Gospel Library.
9. See Russell M. Nelson, comment made at the mission leadership seminar, June 2019; quoted in Dale G. Renlund, "Unwavering Commitment to Jesus Christ," *Ensign* or *Liahona*, Nov. 2019, 25.
10. President Gordon B. Hinckley taught: "When you, as a priest, kneel at the sacrament table and offer up the prayer, which came by revelation, you place the entire congregation under covenant with the Lord. Is this a small thing? It is a most important and remarkable thing" ("The Aaronic Priesthood—a Gift from God," *Ensign*, May 1988, 46).
    "Those who prepare, bless, or pass the sacrament are administering this ordinance to others on behalf of the Lord. Each one who holds the priesthood should approach this assignment with a solemn, reverent attitude. He should be well groomed, clean, and dressed modestly. Personal appearance should reflect the sacredness of the ordinance" ("Priesthood Ordinances and Blessings," *Family Guidebook* [2006], 22).
11. Alma 36:21.
12. Russell M. Nelson, "The Power of Spiritual Momentum," *Liahona*, May 2022, 98.
13. See Mosiah 24:13–15.
14. See John 3:16–17.
15. Alma 26:35–37.

"YE ARE MY FRIENDS"

ELDER DAVID L. BUCKNER
Of the Seventy

In a world filled with contention and division, where civil discourse has been replaced with judgment and scorn, and friendships are defined by -isms and -ites,[1] I have come to know that there is a clear, simple, and divine example we can look to for unity, love, and belonging. That example is Jesus Christ. I testify that He is the great unifier.

We Are His Friends

In December of 1832, as "appearances of troubles among the nations" were becoming "more visible"[2] than at any time since the organization of the Church, Latter-day Saint leaders in Kirtland, Ohio, gathered for a conference. They prayed "separately and vocally to the Lord to reveal his will unto [them]."[3] In acknowledgement of the prayers of these faithful members during times of intense trouble, the Lord comforted them,[4] addressing the Saints three times with two powerful words: "my friends."[5]

Jesus Christ has long called His faithful followers His friends. Fourteen times in the Doctrine and Covenants, the Savior uses the term *friend* to define a sacred and cherished relationship. I am not talking about the word *friend* as the world defines it—subject to social media followers or "likes." It cannot be captured in a hashtag or a number on Instagram or X.

Admittedly, as a teenager, I remember dreaded conversations when I heard those painful words "Hey, can we just be friends?" or "Let's just stay in the friend zone." Nowhere in holy writ do we hear Him say, "Ye are just my friends." Rather, He taught that "greater love hath no man than this, that a man lay down his life for his friends."[6] And "ye are they whom my Father hath given me; ye are my friends."[7]

The sentiment is clear: the Savior numbers each of us and watches over us. This watchcare is not trivial or insignificant. Rather, it is exalting, elevating, and eternal. I see the Savior's declaration "ye are my friends" as a clarion call to build higher and holier[8] relationships among all of God's children "that we may be one."[9] We do this as we come together seeking both opportunities to unite and a sense of belonging for all.

We Are One in Him

The Savior beautifully demonstrated this in His call to "come, follow me."[10] He drew upon the gifts and individual attributes of a diverse group of followers to call His Apostles. He called fishermen,[11] zealots,[12] brothers known for their thunderous personalities,[13] and even a tax collector.[14] Their belief in the Savior and desire to draw unto Him united them. They looked to Him, saw God through Him, and "straightway left their nets, and followed Him."[15]

I too have seen how building higher and holier relationships brings us together as one. My wife, Jennifer, and I were blessed to raise our five children in New York City. There in that busy metropolis, we formed precious and sacred relationships with neighbors, school friends, business associates, faith leaders, and fellow Saints.

In May of 2020, just as the world was grappling with the spread of a global pandemic, members of the New York City Commission of Religious Leaders met virtually in an abruptly called meeting. There was no agenda. No special guests. Just a request to come together and discuss the challenges we were all facing as faith leaders. The Centers for Disease Control had just reported that our city was the epicenter of the COVID-19 pandemic in the United States. This meant no more gathering. No more coming together.

For these religious leaders, removing the personal ministry, the congregational gathering, and the weekly worship was a devastating blow. Our small group—which included a cardinal, reverend, rabbi, imam, pastor, monsignor, and an elder—listened to, consoled, and supported one another. Instead of focusing on our differences, we saw what we had in common. We spoke of possibilities and then probabilities. We rallied and responded to questions about faith and the future. And then we prayed. Oh, how we prayed.

In a richly diverse city filled with complexity and colliding cultures, we saw our differences dissipate as we came together as friends with one voice, one purpose, and one prayer.

No longer were we looking across the table at each other but heavenward with each other. We left each subsequent meeting more united and ready to pick up our "shovels" and go to work. The collaboration that resulted and the service rendered to thousands of New Yorkers taught me that in a world calling for division, distance, and disengagement, there is always much more that unites us than divides us. The Savior pled, "Be one; and if ye are not one ye are not mine."[16]

Brothers and sisters, we must stop looking for reasons to divide and instead seek opportunities to "be one."[17] He has blessed us with unique gifts and attributes that invite learning from one another and personal growth.[18] I often told my university students that if I do what you do and you do what I do, we don't need each other. But because you don't do what I do and I don't do what you do, we do need each other. And that need brings us together. To divide and conquer is the adversary's plan to destroy friendships, families, and faith. It is the Savior who unites.

We Belong to Him

One of the promised blessings of "becoming one" is a powerful sense of belonging. Elder Quentin L. Cook taught that "the essence of truly belonging is to be one with Christ."[19]

On a recent visit with my family to the West African country of Ghana, I was enamored with a local custom. Upon arriving at a church or home, we were greeted with the words "you are welcome." When food was served, our host would announce, "You are invited." These simple greetings were extended with purpose and intentionality. *You are welcome. You are invited.*

We place similar sacred declarations on our meetinghouse doors. But the sign Visitors Welcome is not enough. Do we warmly welcome all who come through the doors? Brothers and sisters, it is not enough to just sit in the pews. We must heed the Savior's call to build higher and holier relationships with all of God's children. We must live our faith! My father often reminded me that simply sitting in a pew on Sunday doesn't make you a good Christian any more than sleeping in a garage makes you a car.

We must live our life so that the world does not see us but sees Him through us. This does not take place only on Sundays. It takes place at the grocery store, the gas pump, the school meeting, the neighborhood gathering—all places where baptized and unbaptized members of our family work and live.

I worship on Sunday as a reminder that we need each other and together we need Him. Our unique gifts and talents that differentiate us in a secular world unite us in a sacred space.[20] The Savior has called upon us to help one another, lift one another, and edify each other. This is what He did when He healed the woman with an issue of blood,[21] cleansed the leper who pled for His mercy,[22] counseled the young prince who asked what more he could do,[23] loved Nicodemus who knew but faltered in his faith,[24] and sat with the woman at the well who did not fit the custom of the day but to whom He declared His messianic mission.[25] This to me is church—a place of gathering and recovery, repair and refocus. As President Russell M. Nelson has taught: "The gospel net is the largest net in the world. God has invited *all* to come unto Him. . . . There is room for everyone."[26]

Some may have had experiences that make you feel you do not belong. The Savior's message to you and me is the same: "Come unto me, all ye that labour and are heavy laden, and I will give you rest."[27] The gospel of Jesus Christ is the perfect place for us. Coming to church offers the hope of better days, the promise that you are not alone, and a family who needs us as much as we need them. Elder D. Todd Christofferson affirms that "being one with the Father, Son, and Holy Spirit is without doubt the ultimate in belonging."[28] To any who have stepped away and are seeking a chance to return, I offer an eternal truth and invitation: You belong. Come back. It is time.

In a contentious and divided world, I testify that the Savior

Jesus Christ is the great unifier. May I invite each of us to be worthy of the Savior's invitation to "be one"[29] and to boldly declare, as He did, "Ye are my friends."[30] In the sacred name of Jesus Christ, amen.

Notes

1. See 4 Nephi 1:17.
2. Doctrine and Covenants 87 section heading.
3. "Minute Book 1," 3, josephsmithpapers.org; spelling modernized.
4. See Doctrine and Covenants 88:3.
5. Doctrine and Covenants 88:3, 62, 117.
6. John 15:13.
7. Doctrine and Covenants 84:63; see also John 15:14.
8. See Russell M. Nelson, "Opening Remarks," *Ensign* or *Liahona*, Nov. 2018, 6.
9. 3 Nephi 19:23; see also John 17:22.
10. Luke 18:22.
11. See Matthew 4:18–22; Mark 1:16–20; Luke 5:2–11; John 1:40–42.
12. See Luke 6:15.
13. See Mark 3:17.
14. See Matthew 9:9–13; Mark 2:13–14; Luke 5:27–32.
15. Matthew 4:20.
16. Doctrine and Covenants 38:27.
17. Doctrine and Covenants 38:27; see also 4 Nephi 1:15–17.
18. See 1 Corinthians 12:12–31; Ephesians 4:3–16.
19. Quentin L. Cook, "Be One with Christ," *Liahona*, May 2024, 51.
20. See 1 Corinthians 12:12–31; Ephesians 4:3–16.
21. See Matthew 9:20–22; Mark 5:25–34; Luke 8:43–48.
22. See Matthew 8:1–4; Mark 1:40–45; Luke 5:12–16.
23. See Matthew 19:16–30; Mark 10:17–31; Luke 18:18–30.
24. See John 3:1–21.
25. See John 4:1–42.
26. Russell M. Nelson, "Peacemakers Needed," *Liahona*, May 2023, 101.
27. Matthew 11:28.
28. D. Todd Christofferson, "The Doctrine of Belonging," *Liahona*, Nov. 2022, 56.
29. Doctrine and Covenants 38:27; see also Doctrine and Covenants 29:13; 35:2; 51:9.
30. John 15:14; Doctrine and Covenants 84:63.

BE THOU CLEAN

ELDER D. MARTIN GOURY
Of the Seventy

When I was about five years old, I was playing football with my friends behind the church in my small village in Côte d'Ivoire. I vividly remember the preacher's call to his congregation to cleanse their clothes in preparation for the Savior's arrival. Being young, I took this call literally. I ran home as fast as my little legs could carry me and begged my mother to clean my few clothes so that I could be spotless and ready for the Savior's coming the next day. Although my mother was skeptical about the Savior's imminent return, she still washed my best outfit.

The next morning, I put on the still slightly damp clothing and eagerly waited for the announcement of the Savior's arrival. As the day wore on and nothing happened, I decided to go to the meeting-house. I was deeply disappointed to find that the church was empty and the Savior had not arrived. You can imagine my feelings as I slowly walked home.

Years later, as I was receiving the missionary lessons in preparation to join The Church of Jesus Christ of Latter-day Saints, I read the following: "And no unclean thing can enter into his kingdom; therefore nothing entereth into his rest save it be those who have washed their garments in my blood, because of their faith, and the repentance of all their sins, and their faithfulness unto the end."[1]

The clarification I received at that time helped me to understand the important truth that had eluded my young mind many years prior. The preacher's message was centered on the importance of spiritual purity. He urged the congregation to seek repentance, make changes in their lives, and turn to the Savior for redemption.

Our Heavenly Father understands our mortal journey and the inevitability of sin in our lives. I am deeply thankful that He has provided a Savior to atone for our transgressions. Through the Savior's redemptive sacrifice, each of us can repent and seek forgiveness and become clean. Repentance, a foundational principle of the gospel, is essential for our spiritual development and resilience as we navigate life's challenges.

During the April 2022 general conference, President Russell M. Nelson invited every member of the Church to experience the joy of daily repentance. He said:

"Please do not fear or delay repenting. Satan delights in your misery. Cut it short. Cast his influence out of your life! Start today to experience the joy of putting off the natural man. The Savior loves us always but *especially* when we repent. . . .

"If you feel you have strayed off the covenant path too far or too long and have no way to return, that simply is not true."[2]

If there is something that you have not fully repented of, I encourage you to heed President Nelson's call not to procrastinate your repentance. It may require some courage to engage in this process; however, I can assure you that the joy that emanates from genuine repentance surpasses understanding. Through repentance, our burdens of guilt are lifted and replaced with a sense of peace and tranquility. As we repent earnestly, we are sanctified through the Savior's blood, increasing our sensitivity to the promptings and influence of the Holy Ghost.

My eternal companion was born with a hearing impairment and as a result must wear hearing aids. Dust and sweat can affect the performance of these devices, and so each morning I observe her diligently cleaning the connecting tubes before wearing the aids. This simple yet consistent routine eliminates any dirt, moisture, or condensation, thereby improving her ability to hear and communicate effectively. When she overlooks this daily ritual, her ability to hear suffers throughout the day; spoken words gradually fade and eventually become inaudible. Just as her daily hearing aid cleaning allows her to hear clearly, daily repentance allows us to discern the guidance of the Lord through the Holy Ghost.

Near the end of the Lord's mortal ministry and before His departure to the Garden of Gethsemane, He prepared His disciples to face the upcoming trials. He assured them, saying, "But the Comforter, which is the Holy Ghost, whom the Father will send in my name, he shall teach you all things, and bring all things to your remembrance, whatsoever I have said unto you."[3]

One of the Holy Ghost's essential functions is to caution, lead, and guide every individual who listens to the soft, inner voice. Just as the blocked communication tubes of a hearing aid can hinder proper functionality, our spiritual connection with our Heavenly Father can also be impaired, leading to dangerous misconceptions or a failure to heed His counsel. The advent of the internet has made information more accessible than ever before. This can lead us to turn to the world for guidance rather than to God. President Russell M. Nelson taught, "In coming days, it will not be possible to survive spiritually without the guiding, directing, comforting, and constant influence of the Holy Ghost."[4]

I am grateful that each of us can receive the gift of the Holy Ghost at the time of our confirmation. However, President Dallin H. Oaks warned that "the blessings available through the gift of the Holy Ghost are conditioned upon worthiness [and] 'the Spirit of the Lord doth not dwell in unholy temples' [Helaman 4:24]."[5]

When we consciously choose to follow the guidance of prophets and apostles, our capacity to have the Holy Ghost as a constant companion grows. The Holy Ghost provides clarity in decision-making, prompting thoughts and impressions that align with our Heavenly Father's will. Having the Holy Ghost as a constant companion is crucial for our spiritual growth.

I was recently assigned to preside over a stake conference at the Salt Lake Granger West Stake in Utah. During this event, I met a stake president who has diligently developed his ability to discern the promptings of the Holy Ghost through righteous living and daily repentance. As part of our ministering efforts, we coordinated visits to three households. Upon completing our final visit, we found ourselves with approximately 30 minutes remaining before our next engagement. As we traveled back to the stake center, President Chesnut received an impression to visit one additional family. We both agreed to follow this prompting.

We proceeded to visit the Jones family,[6] where we discovered

Sister Jones confined to bed due to illness. It was apparent that she needed a priesthood blessing. With her permission, we administered to her. As we prepared to depart, Sister Jones asked how we knew of her urgent need for a blessing. The truth is, *we* didn't know. However, our Heavenly Father, who was aware of her needs, *did* know and inspired President Chesnut to visit her home. When we are receptive to the guidance of the still, small voice, we are better equipped to more effectively minister to those in need.

I testify of a kind and loving Heavenly Father. Jesus Christ is the Savior and Redeemer of mankind. I testify that the Atonement of Jesus Christ is real and that as we learn to follow the guidance of the Holy Ghost, He will lead us to repent and use the power of the Savior's Atonement in our lives. President Russell M. Nelson is the true and living prophet of the Lord, with all priesthood keys on the earth today. In the name of Jesus Christ, amen.

Notes

1. 3 Nephi 27:19.
2. Russell M. Nelson, "The Power of Spiritual Momentum," *Liahona*, May 2022, 98–99.
3. John 14:26.
4. Russell M. Nelson, "Revelation for the Church, Revelation for Our Lives," *Ensign* or *Liahona*, May 2018, 96.
5. Dallin H. Oaks, "Always Have His Spirit," *Ensign*, Nov. 1996, 61.
6. The name *Jones* is not the name of the family visited. I have used a random name for their privacy. I have received written approval from President Chesnut to use his name as well as the name of his stake.

THE WIND DID NEVER CEASE TO BLOW

ELDER AROLDO B. CAVALCANTE
Of the Seventy

In 2015, in the state of Pernambuco, Brazil, 62 members of the J. Reuben Clark Law Society[1] cooperated with the state Prosecutor's Office in investigating the legal challenges of residents in four different nursing homes. For five hours one Saturday, these attorneys interviewed over 200 residents *one by one*, each of whom had been functionally forgotten by society.

During their interviews, they discovered several crimes that had been committed against the elderly residents such as abandonment, mistreatment, and misappropriation of funds. A key pillar of this law society is to care for the poor and in need. Just two months later, the prosecutor successfully filed charges against the responsible parties.

Their assistance is a perfect example of King Benjamin's teaching "that when ye are in the service of your fellow beings ye are only in the service of your God."[2]

One resident I personally interviewed during the pro bono[3] project was a kindhearted 93-year-old woman named Lúcia. Grateful for our service, she jokingly exclaimed, "Marry me!"

Surprised, I responded: "Look over there at that beautiful young woman! She is my wife and the state prosecutor."

She quickly fired back: "So what? She is young, pretty, and can easily get married again. All I have is you!"

The wonderful residents did not have *all* their problems solved that day. They undoubtedly continued to experience hardship from time to time like the Jaredites in their boats on the challenging journey to the promised land, "buried in the depths of the sea, because of the mountain waves which broke upon them."[4]

But that Saturday, the nursing home residents knew that regardless of their earthly anonymity, they were known personally by a loving Heavenly Father, One who responds to even the simplest of prayers.

The Master of masters caused "a furious wind"[5] to blow the Jaredites toward promised blessings. Similarly, we can decide[6] to serve as a humble gust of wind in the Lord's hands. Just as "the wind did never cease to blow"[7] the Jaredites toward the promised land, we can help others progress in their journey to receive God's blessings.

Several years ago, when Chris, my dear wife, and I were interviewed for my calling as bishop, our stake president asked me to prayerfully consider names to recommend as counselors. After hearing the names I recommended, he said I should know a few things about one of the brethren.

First, this brother could not read. Second, he didn't have a car he could use to visit members. Third, he always—*always*—used sunglasses at church. Despite the president's honest concerns, I felt strongly that I should still recommend him as my counselor, and the stake president supported me.

The Sunday my counselors and I were sustained in sacrament meeting, the surprise on the members' faces was evident. This dear brother slowly made his way up to the stand, where the overhead lights reflected brightly across his sunglasses.

As he sat by my side, I asked him, "Brother, do you have problems with your vision?"

"No," he said.

"Then why do you use sunglasses at church?" I asked. "My friend, the members need to see your eyes, and you must be able to see them better too."

In that moment, he took off his sunglasses and never used them at church again.

This beloved brother served at my side until my release as bishop. Today, he continues to serve faithfully in the Church and is an example of dedication and commitment to the Lord Jesus Christ. And yet, years ago, he was an unknown sunglass-wearer sitting essentially forgotten in the pews of the chapel. I often wonder, "How many faithful brothers and sisters sit forgotten among us today?"[8]

Whether we are well-known or forgotten, trials will inevitably come to each one of us.[9] As we turn to the Savior, He can "consecrate

[our] afflictions for [our] gain" and help us respond to our trials in a way that facilitates our spiritual progression.[10] Whether for nursing home residents, a misjudged Church member, or anyone else, we can be "the wind [that] did never cease to blow," bringing hope and guiding others to the covenant path.

Our beloved prophet, President Russell M. Nelson, made an exciting and inspiring invitation to the youth: "I reaffirm strongly that the Lord has asked *every* worthy, able young man to prepare for and serve a mission. For Latter-day Saint young men, missionary service is a priesthood responsibility. . . . For you young and able sisters, a mission is also a powerful, but *optional*, opportunity."[11]

Every day, thousands of young men and women answer the Lord's prophetic call by serving as missionaries. You are brilliant, and as President Nelson has said, you can "have more impact on the world than any previous generation!"[12] Of course, that does not mean you will be the best version of *yourselves* the moment you step foot in the missionary training center.

Instead, you might feel like Nephi, "led by the Spirit, not knowing beforehand the things which [you] should do. Nevertheless [you] went forth."[13]

Perhaps you feel insecure like Jeremiah did and want to say, "I cannot speak: for I am a child."[14]

You might even see your personal shortcomings and want to cry out like Moses did: "O my Lord, I am not eloquent . . . : but I am slow of speech, and of a slow tongue."[15]

If any of you beloved and mighty young men and women is having a thought like this right now, remember that the Lord has answered, "Say not, I am a child: for thou shalt go to all that I shall send thee."[16] And He promises, "Therefore go, and I will be with thy mouth, and teach thee what thou shalt say."[17]

Your transformation from your natural to spiritual self[18] will occur "line upon line, precept upon precept"[19] as you earnestly strive to serve Jesus Christ in the mission field through daily repentance, faith, exact obedience, and hard work[20] to "find constantly, teach repentance, and baptize converts."[21]

Though you wear a name tag, sometimes you may feel unrecognized or forgotten. However, you must know that you have a perfect Heavenly Father, who knows you personally, and a Savior, who loves you. You will have mission leaders who, despite their imperfections, will serve you as "the wind [that] did never cease to blow" in guiding you along your journey of personal conversion.

In the "land that floweth with milk and honey"[22] you will serve in on your mission, you will be spiritually reborn and become a lifelong disciple of Jesus Christ as you draw near to Him.[23] You can come to know that you are never forgotten.

Though some may wait "a long time" for relief, for they "have no man"[24] that can yet help, the Lord Jesus Christ has taught us that no one is ever forgotten by Him. On the contrary, He was a perfect example of seeking out the one in every moment of His mortal ministry.

Each of us—and those around us[25]—faces our own storms of opposition and waves of trials that submerge us daily. But "the wind [will not] cease to blow towards the promised land . . . ; and thus [we shall be] driven forth before the wind."[26]

Each of us can be a part of this wind—the same wind that blessed the Jaredites in their journey and the same wind that, with our help, will bless the unrecognized and forgotten[27] to reach their own promised lands.

I testify that Jesus Christ is our Advocate with the Father. He is a living God and acts as a strong wind that will always guide us along the covenant path. In the name of Jesus Christ, amen.

Notes

1. The J. Reuben Clark Law Society is a nonprofit association formed by lawyers and law students and organized into more than 100 chapters through the world. It was named in honor of Joshua Reuben Clark Jr., who served for many years as a counselor in the First Presidency of The Church of Jesus Christ of Latter-day Saints.
2. Mosiah 2:17.
3. *Pro bono* is the reduced form of the phrase in Latin *pro bono publico*, which means "for the public good" or "for the benefit of the public." This is a form of voluntary work that, unlike traditional volunteering, requires professional qualifications, although it is unpaid.
4. Ether 6:6.
5. Ether 6:5.
6. See 2 Nephi 2:14, 16.
7. Ether 6:8.

8. See Doctrine and Covenants 84:106.

9. See Abraham 3:25.

10. 2 Nephi 2:2; see also Doctrine and Covenants 122:7.

11. Russell M. Nelson, "Preaching the Gospel of Peace," *Liahona*, May 2022, 6.

12. Russel M. Nelson, "Hope of Israel" (worldwide youth devotional, June 3, 2018), Gospel Library.

13. 1 Nephi 4:6–7.

14. Jeremiah 1:6.

15. Exodus 4:10.

16. Jeremiah 1:7.

17. Exodus 4:12.

18. See Mosiah 3:19.

19. 2 Nephi 28:30.

20. See Alma 26:22.

21. Neil L. Andersen, "The Faith to Find and Baptize Converts" (address given at the seminar for new mission presidents, June 25, 2016), 6.

22. See Deuteronomy 11:8–9.

23. See "Becoming Lifelong Disciples of Jesus Christ," *Preach My Gospel: A Guide to Sharing the Gospel of Jesus Christ* (2023), 76–100.

24. John 5:6–7.

25. See Luke 10:29.

26. Ether 6:8.

27. President Dallin H. Oaks mentioned a painting by Maynard Dixon titled *Forgotten Man*, which hangs in his office in the Church Administration Building in Salt Lake City: "You see the sun shining on his head. His Heavenly Father knows he's there. He is forgotten by the passing crowd, but in his struggles, his Heavenly Father knows he's there. . . . I have been with that painting for close to 40 years, and it speaks to me and reminds me of things that I need to remember" (in Sarah Jane Weaver, "What I Learned from President Oaks about the 'Forgotten Man,'" *Church News*, Sept. 18, 2022, thechurchnews.com).

ALIGNING OUR WILL WITH HIS

ELDER ULISSES SOARES
Of the Quorum of the Twelve Apostles

On a certain occasion, the Savior spoke of a merchant man who was searching for "goodly pearls." During the merchant man's search, he found one "of great price." However, in order to acquire the magnificent pearl, this man had to sell all his possessions, which he promptly and joyfully did.[1]

Through this short and thoughtful parable, the Savior beautifully taught that the kingdom of heaven[2] is likened unto a priceless pearl, truly the most precious treasure that should be desired over all else. The fact that the merchant instantly sold all his possessions to obtain that valuable pearl clearly indicates that we should align our mind and desires with the will of the Lord[3] and willingly do everything we can during our mortal journey[4] to attain the eternal blessings of God's kingdom.

To be worthy of this great reward, we certainly need, among other things, to give our best effort to set aside all self-centered pursuits and abandon any entanglement that holds us back from full commitment to the Lord and His higher and holier ways. The Apostle Paul refers to these sanctifying pursuits as "hav[ing] the mind of Christ."[5] As exemplified by Jesus Christ, this means "[doing] always those things that please [the Lord]"[6] in our lives, or as some people say nowadays, this is "doing what works for the Lord."

In a gospel sense, "[doing] always those things that please [the Lord]" relates to submitting our will to His will. The Savior thoughtfully taught the importance of this principle while instructing His disciples:

"For I came down from heaven, not to do mine own will, but the will of him that sent me.

"And this is the Father's will which hath sent me, that of all which he hath given me I should lose nothing, but should raise it up again at the last day.

"And this is the will of him that sent me, that every one which seeth the Son, and believeth on him, may have everlasting life: and I will raise him up at the last day."[7]

The Savior achieved a perfect and divine level of submission to the Father by allowing His will to be swallowed up in the Father's will.[8] He once said, "And he that sent me is with me: the Father hath not left me alone; for I do always those things that please him."[9] In teaching the Prophet Joseph Smith about the anguish and agonies of the Atonement, the Savior said:

"For behold, I, God, have suffered these things for all, that they might not suffer if they would repent; . . .

"Which suffering caused myself, even God, the greatest of all, to tremble because of pain, and to bleed at every pore, and to suffer both body and spirit—and would that I might not drink the bitter cup, and shrink—

"Nevertheless, glory be to the Father, and I partook and finished my preparations unto the children of men."[10]

During our sojourn in mortality, we often wrestle with what we think we know, what we think is best, and what we assume works for us, as opposed to comprehending what Heavenly Father actually knows, what is eternally best, and what absolutely works for children within His plan. This great wrestle can become very complex, especially considering the prophecies contained in the scriptures for our day: "This know also, that in the last days . . . men shall be lovers of their own selves, . . . lovers of pleasures more than lovers of God."[11]

One sign that indicates fulfillment of this prophecy is the current growing trend in the world, adopted by so many, of people becoming consumed with themselves and constantly proclaiming, "No matter what, I live my own truth or I do what works for me." As Paul the Apostle said, they "seek their own, not the things which are Jesus Christ's."[12] This way of thinking is often justified as being "authentic" by those who indulge in self-centered pursuits, focus on personal preferences, or want to justify certain types of behavior that frequently don't match God's loving plan and His will for them. If we let our heart and mind embrace this way of thinking, we can create significant stumbling blocks for ourselves in acquiring the most priceless pearl that God has lovingly prepared for His children—eternal life.[13]

While it is true that each of us travels an individualized discipleship journey on the covenant path, striving to keep our hearts and minds centered on Christ Jesus,[14] we need to be careful and constantly vigilant to not be tempted[15] to adopt this type of worldly philosophy in our life. Elder Quentin L. Cook said that "being sincerely Christlike is an even more important goal than being authentic."[16]

My dear friends, when we choose to let God be the most powerful influence in our life over our self-serving pursuits, we can make progress in our discipleship and increase our capacity to unite our mind and heart with the Savior. On the other hand, when we don't allow God's way to prevail in our life, we are left to ourselves, and without the Lord's inspiring guidance, we can justify almost anything we do or don't do. We can also make excuses for ourselves by doing things our own way, saying in effect, "I am just doing things my way."

On one occasion, while the Savior was declaring His doctrine, some people, particularly self-righteous Pharisees, rejected His message and boldly declared that they were children of Abraham, implying that their lineage would grant them special privileges in the sight of God. That mentality led them to lean unto their own understanding and to disbelieve what the Savior was teaching. The Pharisees' reaction to Jesus was clear evidence that their presumptuous attitude left no place in their hearts for the Savior's words and God's way. In response, Jesus wisely and courageously declared that if they were true covenant children of Abraham, they would do the works of Abraham, especially considering that the God of Abraham was standing before them and teaching them the truth at that very moment.[17]

Brothers and sisters, as you can see, acting on these mental gymnastics of "what works for me" versus doing "what always pleases the Lord" is not a new trend that is unique to our day. It is an age-old mentality that has crossed the centuries and often blinds the wise-in-their-own-eyes[18] and confuses and exhausts many of God's children. This mentality is, in fact, an old trick of the adversary; it is a deceptive path that carefully leads God's children away from the true and faithful covenant path.[19] While personal circumstances such as genetics, geography, and physical and mental challenges do influence our journey, in things that truly matter, there is an inner space where we are free to choose[20] whether or not we will decide to follow the pattern the Lord has prepared for our life. Truly, "He marked the path and led the way, and ev'ry point [defined]."[21]

As Christ's disciples, we desire to walk the path He marked for us during His mortal ministry. We not only desire to do His will and all that will please Him but also seek to emulate Him. As we strive to be true to every covenant we have entered into and live "by every word that proceedeth out of the mouth of God,"[22] we will be protected against falling victim to the sins and errors of the world—errors of philosophy and doctrine that would lead us away from those most precious pearls.

I have been personally inspired by how such spiritual submissiveness to God has impacted the lives of faithful disciples of Christ as they chose to do those things that work for and are pleasing in the sight of the Lord. I know a young man who was unsettled about going on a mission but felt inspired to go and serve the Lord when he listened to a senior leader of the Church sharing his own personal testimony and sacred experience of serving as a missionary.

In his own words, this young man, now a returned missionary, said: "As I listened to the testimony of an Apostle of the Savior Jesus Christ, I was able to feel of God's love for me, and I desired to share that love with others. At that moment I knew that I should serve a mission despite my fears, doubts, and concerns. I felt totally confident in the blessings and promises of God for His children. Today, I am a new person; I have a testimony that this gospel is true and that the Church of Jesus Christ has been restored on earth." This young man chose the Lord's way and became an example of a true disciple in every aspect.

A faithful young woman decided not to compromise her standards when she was asked to dress immodestly to fit into the business division of the fashion company where she worked. Understanding that her body is a sacred gift from our Heavenly Father and a place where the Spirit can dwell, she was moved to live by a standard higher than the world's. She not only gained the confidence of those who saw her living by the truth of the gospel of Jesus Christ but also preserved her job, which for a moment was in jeopardy. Her willingness to do what was pleasing in the sight of the Lord, rather than what worked for the world, gave her covenant confidence amidst difficult choices.

Brothers and sisters, we are constantly confronted by similar decisions in our daily journey. It takes a courageous and a willing heart to pause and pursue an honest and meek introspection to acknowledge the presence of weaknesses of the flesh in our life that may impede our ability to submit ourselves to God, and ultimately decide to adopt His way rather than our own. The ultimate test of our discipleship is found in our willingness to give up and lose our old self and submit our heart and our whole soul to God so that His will becomes ours.

One of the most glorious moments of mortality occurs when we discover the joy that comes when doing always those things that "work for and please the Lord" and "what works for us" become one and the same! To decisively and unquestioningly make the Lord's will our own requires majestic and heroic discipleship! At that sublime moment, we become consecrated to the Lord, and we totally yield our wills to Him.[23] Such spiritual submissiveness, so to speak, is beautiful, powerful, and transformational.

I testify to you that following the Lord's will in our life will enable us to find the most precious pearl in the world—the kingdom of heaven. I pray that each of us, in our time and turn, will be able to declare, with covenant confidence, to our Heavenly Father and Savior Jesus Christ that "what works for Thee, works for me." I say these things in the sacred name of the Savior Jesus Christ, amen.

Notes

1. See Matthew 13:45–46.
2. See Guide to the Scriptures, "Kingdom of God or Kingdom of Heaven" and "Eternal Life," Gospel Library.
3. See Doctrine and Covenants 68:4.
4. See Guide to the Scriptures, "Endure," Gospel Library.
5. 1 Corinthians 2:16; see also Philippians 4:1.
6. John 8:29; see also 1 John 3:22.
7. John 6:38–40.
8. See Mosiah 15:7.
9. John 8:29.
10. Doctrine and Covenants 19:16, 18–19.
11. 2 Timothy 3:1–2, 4.
12. Philippians 2:21.
13. See Guide to the Scriptures, "Eternal Life," Gospel Library.
14. See Philippians 4:7; Doctrine and Covenants 43:34.
15. See Guide to the Scriptures, "Tempt, Temptation," Gospel Library.
16. Quentin L. Cook, "'Fear Not . . . in Me Your Joy Is Full' (D&C 101:36)" (worldwide devotional for young adults, Sept. 11, 2016), Gospel Library.
17. See Proverbs 3:5; John 8:33–42; see also the works of Abraham: Abraham converted others to the gospel (Genesis 12:5); he avoided strife (Genesis 13:7–9); he was obedient to God (Genesis 12:1–9; 15:1–6; 22:1–19); he welcomed heavenly messengers (Genesis 18:1–8); and he exercised tremendous faith (Genesis 22:1–19).
18. See Proverbs 3:5–7.
19. See 2 Nephi 28:21–23, 26.
20. See Guide to the Scriptures, "Agency," Gospel Library.
21. "How Great the Wisdom and the Love," Hymns, no. 195.
22. Matthew 4:4.
23. See Guide to the Scriptures, "Consecrate, Law of Consecration," Gospel Library.

Saturday Evening Session

OCTOBER 5, 2024

HOLINESS TO THE LORD IN EVERYDAY LIFE

ELDER GERRIT W. GONG
Of the Quorum of the Twelve Apostles

Our recent Gong family reunion included a fun talent show, complete with a dad jokes contest.

But this contest was unusual. On one team was Grandpa (me) and two of the grandchildren, ages 12 and 11. On the other team was an artificial intelligence (AI) program prompted by a cousin to tell dad jokes in the style of Gerrit W. Gong. Grandpa Gerrit Gong versus AI Gerrit Gong.

The grandchildren and I went first.

What do you call a dinosaur who crashes his car? Tyrannosaurus Wrecks.

AI Gerrit Gong was instructed—think like Gerrit W. Gong. Talk like him.

AI Gerrit Gong—"Here is a dad joke as if spoken by Gerrit W. Gong, embracing his warm, thoughtful, and uplifting style: Why did the humble tree make people smile? Because it was rooted in love and reached out with branches of kindness. Like that tree, we too can find strength in our roots and joy in extending kindness to others."

Well, what do you think? That's why they're called dad jokes.

All around us are opportunities to laugh, delight, see with grateful eyes. Ours is a gospel of joy and holiness in everyday life. Holiness sets things apart for sacred purpose. But holiness also invites us to infuse daily living with the sacred—to rejoice in daily bread amidst this world's thistles and thorns. To walk with the Lord, we must become holy, for He is holy,[1] and to help us become holy, the Lord invites us to walk with Him.[2]

We each have a story. As Sister Gong and I meet you—Church members and friends in many places and circumstances—your stories of holiness to the Lord in everyday life inspire us. You live seven Cs: communion with God, community and compassion with each other, commitment and covenant with God, family, and friends—centered in Jesus Christ.

Growing evidence highlights this striking fact: religious believers are on average happier, healthier, and more fulfilled than those without spiritual commitment or connection. Happiness and life satisfaction, mental and physical health, meaning and purpose, character and virtue, close social relationships, even financial and material stability—on each measure, religious practitioners flourish.[3]

They enjoy better physical and mental health and greater life satisfaction across all ages and demographic groups.

What researchers call "religious structural stability" offers clarity, purpose, and inspiration amidst life's twists and turns. The household of faith and community of Saints combat isolation and the lonely crowd. Holiness to the Lord says no to the profane, no to snarky cleverness at others' expense, no to algorithms that monetize anger and polarization. Holiness to the Lord says yes to the sacred and reverent, yes to our becoming our freest, happiest, most authentic, best selves as we follow Him in faith.

What does holiness to the Lord in everyday life look like?

Holiness to the Lord in everyday life looks like two faithful young adults, married for a year, sharing with authenticity and vulnerability gospel covenants, sacrifice, and service in their unfolding lives.[4]

She begins, "In high school, I was in a dark place. I felt like God wasn't there for me. One night, a text from a friend said, 'Hey, have you read Alma 36 ever?'

"As I started reading," she said, "I was overcome with peace and love. I felt like I was being given this big hug. When I read Alma 36:12, I knew Heavenly Father saw me and knew exactly how I was feeling."

She continues, "Before we got married, I was honest with my fiancé that I didn't have a great testimony of tithing. Why did God need us to give money when others had so much to give? My fiancé helped explain it's not about money but following a commandment asked of us. He challenged me to start paying tithing.

"I really saw my testimony grow," she said. "Sometimes money gets tight, but we saw so many blessings, and somehow paychecks were enough."

Also, "in my nursing class," she said, "I was the only member of the Church and the only one married. Many times I left class frustrated or crying because I felt classmates singled me out and made negative comments about my beliefs, my wearing my garments, or my being married so young."

Yet she continues, "This past semester I learned how to better voice my beliefs and be a good gospel example. My knowledge and testimony grew because I was tested in my ability to stand alone and be strong in what I believe."

The young husband adds, "Before my mission I had offers to play college baseball. Making the difficult decision, I put those offers aside and went to serve the Lord. I wouldn't trade those two years for anything.

"Returning home," he said, "I expected a difficult transition but found myself stronger, faster, and healthier. I was throwing harder than when I left. I had more offers to play than when I left, including my dream school. And, most importantly," he said, "I rely upon the Lord more than ever."

He concludes, "As a missionary I taught that Heavenly Father promises us power in our prayers, but sometimes I forget that for myself."[5]

Our treasury of missionary holiness-to-the-Lord blessings is rich and full.[6] Finances, timing, and other circumstances are often not easy. But when missionaries of all ages and backgrounds consecrate holiness to the Lord, things can work out in the Lord's time and way.

Now with a 48-year perspective, a senior missionary shares, "My dad wanted me to get a college education, not go on a mission. Shortly after that, he had a heart attack and died at age 47. I felt guilty. How could I make things right with my father?

"Later," he continues, "after I decided to serve a mission, I saw my father in a dream. Peaceful and contented, he was happy I would serve."

This senior missionary continues, "As Doctrine and Covenants section 138 teaches, I believe my father could serve as a missionary in the spirit world. I picture my father helping our great-grandfather, who left Germany at age 17 and was lost to the family, be found again."

His wife adds, "Among the five brothers in my husband's family, the four who served missions are the ones with college degrees."

Holiness to the Lord in everyday life looks like a young returning missionary who learned to let God prevail in his life. Earlier, when asked to bless someone who was very sick, this missionary said, "I have faith; I will bless him to recover. Yet," the returning missionary says, "I learned in that moment to pray not for what I wanted but for what the Lord knew the person needed. I blessed the brother with peace and comfort. He later passed away peacefully."

Holiness to the Lord in everyday life feels like a spark arcing across the veil to connect, comfort, and strengthen. An administrator at a major university says he feels individuals he knows only by reputation praying for him. Those individuals devoted their lives to the university and continue to care about its mission and students.

A sister does her best each day, after her husband was unfaithful to her and the children. I deeply admire her and others like her. One day while folding laundry, her hand on a stack of garments, she sighed to herself, "What's the point?" She felt a tender voice assure her, "Your covenants are with me."[7]

For 50 years, another sister yearned for a relationship with her father.[8] "Growing up," she says, "there were my brothers and my dad, and then there was me—the only daughter. All I ever wanted was to be 'good enough' for my dad.

"Then my mom passed away! She was my only liaison between my dad and me.

"One day," the sister said, "I heard a voice say, 'Invite your dad and take him to the temple with you.' That was the beginning of a twice-a-month date with my daddy to the house of the Lord. I told my dad I loved him. He told me he loved me too.

"Spending time in the house of the Lord has healed us. My mom could not help us on earth. It took her being on the other side of the veil to help mend what was broken. The temple completed our journey to wholeness as an eternal family."

The father says, "The temple dedication was a great spiritual experience for me and my only daughter. Now we attend together and feel our love strengthen."

Holiness to the Lord in everyday life includes tender moments when loved ones pass. Earlier this year, my dear mother, Jean Gong, slipped into the next life days before her 98th birthday.[9]

If you asked my mother, "Would you like rocky road, white chocolate ginger, or strawberry ice cream?" Mom would say, "Yes, please, may I taste each one?" Who could say no to your mother, especially when she loved all of life's flavors?

I once asked Mom which decisions had most shaped her life.

She said, "Being baptized a member of The Church of Jesus Christ of Latter-day Saints and moving from Hawaii to the mainland, where I met your father."

Baptized as a 15-year-old, the only member of her large family to join our Church, my mother had covenant faith and trust in the Lord that blessed her life and all our family generations. I miss my mother, as you miss members in your family. But I know my mother is not gone. She is just not here now. I honor her and all who pass as valiant examples of everyday holiness to the Lord.

Of course, holiness to the Lord in everyday life includes coming more often to the Lord in His holy house.[10] This is true whether we are Church members or friends.

Three friends came to the Bangkok Thailand Temple open house.

"This is a place of super healing," said one.

In the baptistry, another said, "When I am here, I want to be washed clean and never sin again."

The third said, "Can you feel the spiritual power?"

With nine sacred words, our temples invite and proclaim:
"Holiness to the Lord.
"The House of the Lord."[11]

Holiness to the Lord makes daily living sacred. It draws us closer and happier to the Lord and each other and prepares us to live with God our Father, Jesus Christ, and our loved ones.

As did my friend, you may wonder if your Heavenly Father loves you. The answer is a resounding, absolute yes! We can feel His love as we make holiness to the Lord ours each day, happy and forever. May we do so, I pray in the sacred name of Jesus Christ, amen.

Notes

1. From Old Testament times, we are taught, "Ye shall therefore sanctify yourselves, and ye shall be holy; for I am holy" (Leviticus 11:44). We are to walk in holiness before the Lord (see Doctrine and Covenants 20:69), stand in holy places (see Doctrine and Covenants 45:32), keep the Sabbath day holy (see Exodus 20:8), wear holy garments (see Exodus 29:29), use holy anointing oil (see Exodus 30:25), be blessed by holy prophets (see Doctrine and Covenants 10:46), and rely upon holy scriptures (see Doctrine and Covenants 20:11), holy laws (see Doctrine and Covenants 20:20), and holy angels (see Doctrine and Covenants 20:6). Holiness to the Lord is intended to bless all aspects of our daily life.
2. See Moses 6:34.
3. See "Religion and Spirituality: Tools for Better Wellbeing?," Gallup Blog, Oct. 10, 2023, news.gallup.com. "Worldwide, people with a greater commitment to spirituality or religion have better wellbeing in many respects"—including positive emotions, sense of purpose, community engagement, and social connections (*Faith and Wellness: The Worldwide Connection between Spirituality and Wellbeing* [2023], 4, faithandmedia.com/research/gallup).
4. Each quoted experience is shared—with my admiration and appreciation—in the words of the individuals involved and by their permission.
5. Today in the Church, young adults ages 18–35 (including both young single and young married adults) and single adults (ages 36–45) constitute one-third (32.5 percent) of total Church members. Of those 5.623 million Church members, young adults ages 18–35 total in number 3.625 million (of which 694,000 are married), and single adults ages 36–45 total in number 1.998 million. Our young and single adults are outstanding; each one is precious. Each has an individual story of faith, seeking, resilience, and compassion. The example shared here is representative of the remarkable range of stories and experience young and single adults share as I meet you in many settings and circumstances across the Church.
6. Currently, some 77,500 missionaries are serving in 450 missions worldwide. This includes young teaching missionaries, young service missionaries, and senior couples, but not 27,800 senior service missionaries and long-term volunteers. Each missionary story, from preparation through service and return, is individual and full of holiness to the Lord in personal experience.

   Many missionary experiences reflect a spiritual pattern. This includes individual testimony of selfless inviting and helping others to come to Jesus Christ and of the missionary becoming a disciple of Jesus Christ and *Preach My Gospel* missionary. *Preach My Gospel* missionaries are changed, even transformed, by their testimony experiences. They learn to love individuals, places, languages, and cultures. They fulfill prophecy by bringing the glad tidings of the fulness of the restored gospel of Jesus Christ to nations, kindreds, and peoples. They find good in and learn to live with every companion. They work with members, leaders, and friends in many circumstances and backgrounds, and so much more.

   Preach My Gospel missionaries nurture faith and confidence. They build consecrated companionships. They learn that obedience brings blessings and miracles. In a myriad other personalized ways, they truly become and know by covenant: "I am a disciple of Jesus Christ, the Son of God" (3 Nephi 5:13).

7. Some of our most faithful and courageous Church members, sisters and brothers, find themselves facing situations they never expected and never would have chosen. These true Saints carry on, day in and day out, often waiting on the Lord. The Lord is aware of each and, as this example tenderly shares, desires to encourage and strengthen each of us in His time and way.

8. There is much longing for relationships with parents and children. I am deeply grateful for each situation in which, even after many years, reconciliation, forgiveness, and covenant belonging are created or restored. This good sister does not want anyone to think poorly of her father. She says, "He is a fine and faithful leader and a good father."

9. A paradox of parenting is that children are deeply shaped by how they are nurtured, yet they usually remember little of the early years when their mothers tirelessly, selflessly mother. Words are insufficient to express the truism that my understanding, love, and appreciation for my father and mother expanded and deepened as I became a husband, parent, and grandparent. Reflecting the generational nature of the plan of happiness, we can, in temple mirrors of eternity, see ourselves as a mother, grandmother, great-grandmother in one direction and as a daughter, granddaughter, great-granddaughter in the other direction.

10. Today, approximately 60 percent of Church members worldwide live within 50 miles (80 km, or about an hour travel time in many places) of a house of the Lord. In coming years, as announced temples are completed, approximately three-fourths of Church members will live within an hour of a house of the Lord. Depending on circumstances, that is hopefully close enough to come often to the Lord in His holy house, thereby blessing generations of precious family members and ourselves and our posterity.

11. On our temples, the standard inscription is "Holiness to the Lord, the House of the Lord." A few temples include more than this inscription, such as adding the name of the Church. A few temples have the inscription reversed: "The House of the Lord, Holiness to the Lord" (in Atlanta, Los Angeles, and San Diego in the United States). The Logan Utah Temple inscription simply states, "Holiness to the Lord."

THE JOY OF OUR REDEMPTION

SISTER KRISTIN M. YEE

Second Counselor in the Relief Society General Presidency

About 10 years ago I felt impressed to paint a portrait of the Savior. Though I am an artist, this felt a bit overwhelming. How was *I* to paint a portrait of Jesus Christ that captured His Spirit? Where was I to begin? And where would I find the time?

Even with my questions, I decided to move forward and trust that the Lord would help me. But I had to keep moving and leave the *possibilities* to Him.[1] I prayed, pondered, researched, and sketched and was blessed to find help and resources. And what was a white canvas started to become something more.

The process wasn't easy. Sometimes it didn't look as I had hoped. Sometimes there were moments of inspired strokes and ideas. And many times, I just had to try again and again and again.

When I thought the oil painting was finally complete and dry, I began to apply a transparent varnish to protect it from dirt and dust. As I did, I noticed the hair in the painting start to change, smear, and dissolve. I quickly realized that I had applied the varnish too soon, that part of the painting was still wet!

I had literally wiped away a portion of my painting with the varnish. Oh, how my heart sank. I felt as though I had just destroyed what God had helped me to do. I cried and felt sick inside. In despair, I did what anyone would typically do in a situation like this: I called my mother. She wisely and calmly said, "You won't get back what you had, but do the very best you can with what you've got."

So I prayed and pled for help and painted through the night to repair things. And I remember looking at the painting in the morning—it looked better than it did before. How was that possible? What I thought was a mistake without mend was an opportunity for His merciful hand to be manifest. He was not done with the painting, and He was not done with me.[2] What joy and relief filled my heart. I praised the Lord for His mercy, for this miracle that not only saved the painting but taught me more about His love and power to save each of us from our mistakes, weaknesses, and sins and to help us become something more.

Just as the depth of my gratitude for the Savior grew as He mercifully helped me to repair the "unrepairable" painting, so has my personal love and gratitude for my Savior intensified as I've sought to work with Him on my weaknesses and to be forgiven of my mistakes. I will forever be grateful to my Savior that I can change[3] and be cleansed.[4] He has my heart, and I hope to do whatever He would have me do and become.

Repenting allows us to feel God's love and to know and love Him in ways we would never otherwise know.[5] Of the woman who anointed the Savior's feet, He said, "Her sins, which are many, are forgiven; for she loved much: but to whom little is forgiven, the same loveth little."[6] She loved Jesus much, for He had forgiven her much.

There is such relief and hope in knowing that we *can* try again—that, as Elder David A. Bednar taught, we can receive an ongoing remission of our sins through the sanctifying power of the Holy Ghost as we truly and sincerely repent.[7]

The redeeming power of Jesus Christ is one of the greatest promised blessings of our covenants. Ponder this as you participate in sacred ordinances.[8] Without it, we could not return home to the presence of our Father in Heaven and those we love.

I know that our Lord and Savior, Jesus Christ, is mighty to save. As the Son of God, who atoned for the sins of the world and laid down His own life[9] and took it up again, He holds the power of redemption and resurrection.[10] He has made possible immortality for all and eternal life for those who choose Him. I know that through His atoning sacrifice, we can repent and truly be cleansed and redeemed.[11] It is a miracle He loves you and me in this way.[12]

He has said, "Will ye not now return unto me, and repent of your sins, and be converted, that I may heal you?"[13] He can heal[14] the "waste places" of your soul—the places made dry, harsh, and desolate by sin and sorrow—and "make [your] wilderness like Eden."[15]

Just as we cannot comprehend the agony and depth of Christ's suffering in Gethsemane and on the cross, so we "cannot measure the bounds nor fathom the depths of [His] divine forgiveness,"[16] mercy, and love.[17]

You may feel at times that it's not possible to be redeemed, that perhaps you are an exception to God's love and the Savior's atoning power because of what you are struggling with or because of what you've done. But I testify that you are not beneath the Master's reach. The Savior "descended below all things"[18] and is in a divine position to lift you and claim you from the darkest abyss and bring you into "his marvellous light."[19] Through His sufferings, He has made a way for each of us to overcome our personal weaknesses and sins. "He has *all* power to save *every* man that believeth on his name and bringeth forth fruit meet for repentance."[20]

Just as it required work and pleading for heaven's help to repair the painting, it takes work, sincerity of heart, and humility to bring "forth fruit meet for repentance." These fruits include exercising our faith and trust in Jesus Christ and His atoning sacrifice,[21] offering to God a broken heart and a contrite spirit,[22] confessing and forsaking sin,[23] restoring that which has been damaged to the best of our ability,[24] and striving to live righteously.[25]

To truly repent and change, we must first be "convinced of our sins."[26] A person does not see the need to take medicine unless they understand that they are ill.[27] There may be times we may not be willing to look inside ourselves and see that which really needs healing and repair.

In C. S. Lewis's writings, Aslan poses these words to a man who has entangled himself in his own devices: "Oh [humankind], how cleverly you defend yourselves [from] all that might do you good!"[28]

Where might you and I be defending ourselves from those things that might do us good?

Let us not defend ourselves from the good that God desires to bless us with. From the love and mercy that He desires us to feel.[29] From the light and knowledge He desires to bestow upon us.[30] From the healing that He knows we so readily need. From the deeper covenant relationship He intends for all His sons and daughters.[31]

I pray we may lay aside any "weapons of war"[32] that we've consciously or even unconsciously taken up to defend ourselves from the blessings of God's love. Weapons of pride, selfishness, fear, hate, offense, complacency, unrighteous judgment, jealousies[33]—anything that would keep us from loving God with *all* our hearts and keeping *all* our covenants with Him.

As we live our covenants, the Lord can give us the help and power we need to both recognize[34] and overcome our weaknesses, including the spiritual parasite of pride. Our prophet has said:

"Repentance is the pathway to purity, and purity brings power."[35]

"And oh, how we will need His power in the days ahead."[36]

Like my painting, the Lord is not done with us when we make a mistake, nor does He flee when we falter. Our need for healing and help is not a burden to Him, but the very reason He came. The Savior Himself said:

"Behold, I have come unto the world to bring redemption unto the world, to save the world from sin."[37]

"Mine arm of mercy is extended towards you, and whosoever will come, him will I receive; and blessed are those who come unto me."[38]

So come—come ye that are weary, worn, and sad; come and leave your labors and find rest in Him who loves you most. Take His yoke upon you, for He is gentle and lowly in heart.[39]

Our Heavenly Father and Savior see you. They know your heart. They care about what you care about, including those you love.

The Savior can redeem that which was lost, including broken and fractured relationships. He has made a way for all that is fallen to be redeemed—to breathe life into that which feels dead and hopeless.[40]

If you are struggling with a situation you think you should have overcome by now, don't give up. Be patient with yourself, keep your covenants, repent often, seek the help of your leaders if needed, and go to the house of the Lord as regularly as you can.[41] Listen for and heed the promptings He sends you. He will not abandon His covenant relationship with you.[42]

There have been difficult and complex relationships in my life that I have struggled with and sincerely sought to improve. At times I felt like I was failing more often than not. I wondered, "Did I not fix things the last time? Did I not truly overcome my weakness?" I've learned over time that I am not necessarily defective; rather, there is often more to work on and more healing that is needed.[43]

Elder D. Todd Christofferson taught: "Surely the Lord smiles upon one who desires to come to judgment worthily, who resolutely labors day by day to replace weakness with strength. Real repentance, real change may require repeated attempts, but there is something refining and holy in such striving. Divine forgiveness and healing flow quite naturally to such a soul."[44]

Each day is a new day filled with hope and possibilities because of Jesus Christ. Each day you and I can come to know, as Mother Eve proclaimed, "the joy of our redemption,"[45] the joy of being made whole, the joy of feeling God's unfailing love for you.

I know that our Father in Heaven and Savior love you. Jesus Christ is the Savior and Redeemer of all mankind. He lives. Through His atoning sacrifice, the bands of sin and death were *forever* broken so that we might be *free* to choose healing, redemption, and eternal life with those we love.[46] And I testify of these things in His name, Jesus Christ, amen.

Notes

1. See Matthew 19:26.
2. "Once we make a covenant with God, we leave neutral ground forever. God will not abandon His relationship with those who have forged such a bond with Him. In fact, all those who have made a covenant with God have access to a special kind of love and mercy. In the Hebrew language, that covenantal love is called *hesed* (חֶסֶד)" (Russell M. Nelson, "The Everlasting Covenant," *Liahona*, Oct. 2022, 5).
3. "When you and I also enter that path, we have a new way of life. We thereby create a relationship with God that allows Him to bless and change us. The covenant path leads us back to Him. If we let God prevail in our lives, that covenant will lead us closer and closer to Him. All covenants are intended to be binding. They create a relationship with everlasting ties" (Russell M. Nelson, "The Everlasting Covenant," 5).
4. See Alma 26:35–36.
5. See Alma 22:18: "I will give away all my sins to know thee."
6. Luke 7:47; see also verses 37–50.
7. Speaking of the sacrament, Elder David A. Bednar said:
   "As we prepare conscientiously and participate in this holy ordinance with a broken heart and a contrite spirit, then the promise is that we may *always* have the Spirit of the Lord to be with us. And by the sanctifying power of the Holy Ghost as our constant companion, we can

always retain a remission of our sins" ("Always Retain a Remission of Your Sins," *Ensign* or *Liahona*, May 2016, 61–62).

"In the process of coming unto the Savior and spiritual rebirth, receiving the sanctifying power of the Holy Ghost in our lives creates the possibility of an *ongoing cleansing* of our soul from sin. This joyous blessing is vital because 'no unclean thing can dwell with God' [1 Nephi 10:21]" ("Always Retain a Remission of Your Sins," 61).

Elder Bednar taught at the 2023 mission leadership seminar: "And by the sanctifying power of the Holy Ghost as our constant companion, we can always retain a remission of our sins. Thus, the gospel of Jesus Christ provides second, and third, and fourth, and endless opportunities to retain a remission of our sins" (in Rachel Sterzer Gibson, "Teach to Build Faith in Jesus Christ, Elder Bednar Instructs," *Church News*, June 23, 2023, thechurchnews.com).

8. "The Prophet Joseph Smith summarized succinctly the essential role of priesthood ordinances in the gospel of Jesus Christ: 'Being born again, comes by the Spirit of God through ordinances' [*Teachings of Presidents of the Church: Joseph Smith* (2007), 95]. This penetrating statement emphasizes the roles of both the Holy Ghost and sacred ordinances in the process of spiritual rebirth. . . .

"Holy ordinances are central in the Savior's gospel and in the process of coming unto Him and seeking spiritual rebirth. . . .

"The ordinances of salvation and exaltation administered in the Lord's restored Church are far more than rituals or symbolic performances. Rather, they constitute authorized channels through which the blessings and powers of heaven can flow into our individual lives. . . .

"Ordinances received and honored with integrity are essential to obtaining the power of godliness and all of the blessings made available through the Savior's Atonement" (David A. Bednar, "Always Retain a Remission of Your Sins," 59–60).

9. See John 10:17–18; 3 Nephi 9:22.
10. See Joseph Smith Translation, John 1:16; Jacob 6:9; Moses 1:39.
11. See Alma 12:33–34.
12. See John 3:16.
13. 3 Nephi 9:13.
14. "I plead with you to come unto Him so that He can . . . heal you from sin as you repent. He will heal you from sadness and fear. He will heal you from the wounds of this world" (Russell M. Nelson, "The Answer Is Always Jesus Christ," *Liahona*, May 2023, 127).
15. Isaiah 51:3; see also Isaiah 58:10–12; Ezekiel 36:33–36.
16. James E. Talmage, *Jesus the Christ* (1916), 265.
17. See Russell M. Nelson, "The Everlasting Covenant," 5–7; see also endnotes 2 and 3 in this message.
18. Doctrine and Covenants 88:6; see also Doctrine and Covenants 122:7–9.
19. 1 Peter 2:9; see also Alma 26:16–17.
20. Alma 12:15; emphasis added.
21. See Alma 34:17.
22. See 2 Corinthians 7:10; 3 Nephi 9:15–22.
23. See Doctrine and Covenants 58:43; 64:7.
24. See Mosiah 27:32–37; Alma 26:30.
25. See Doctrine and Covenants 1:32.
26. See Alma 24:8–10.
27. See Robert L. Millet, *Becoming New: A Doctrinal Commentary on the Writings of Paul* (2022), 26.
28. C. S. Lewis, *The Magician's Nephew* (1955), 185.
29. See Mosiah 4:6–9.
30. See Alma 12:9–10; 26:22; 3 Nephi 26:9.
31. "The covenant path is all about our relationship with God" (Russell M. Nelson, "The Everlasting Covenant," 11; see also endnotes 2 and 3 in this message).
32. See Alma 24:17–19.
33. See Doctrine and Covenants 67:10.
34. See Jacob 4:13. "Those who do not see their weaknesses do not progress. Your awareness of your weakness is a blessing as it helps you remain humble and keeps you turning to the Savior. The Spirit not only comforts you, but He is also the agent by which the Atonement works a change

in your very nature. Then weak things become strong" (Henry B. Eyring, "My Peace I Leave with You," *Ensign* or *Liahona*, May 2017, 16).

35. Russell M. Nelson, "We Can Do Better and Be Better," *Ensign* or *Liahona*, May 2019, 68.

36. "Everything taught in the temple, through instruction and through the Spirit, increases our understanding of Jesus Christ. His essential ordinances bind us to Him through sacred priesthood covenants. Then, as we keep our covenants, He endows us with *His* healing, strengthening power. And oh, how we will need His power in the days ahead" (Russell M. Nelson, "The Temple and Your Spiritual Foundation," *Liahona*, Nov. 2021, 93–94).

37. 3 Nephi 9:21.

38. 3 Nephi 9:14.

39. See Erik Dewar, "Come Find His Rest" (song, 2024); see also Matthew 11:28–30.

40. See Deuteronomy 30:20; John 11:25; Ether 3:14; Doctrine and Covenants 88:6, 13.

41. "My dear brothers and sisters, here is my promise. Nothing will help you *more* to hold fast to the iron rod than worshipping in the temple as regularly as your circumstances permit. Nothing will protect you *more* as you encounter the world's mists of darkness. Nothing will bolster your testimony of the Lord Jesus Christ and His Atonement or help you understand God's magnificent plan *more*. Nothing will soothe your spirit *more* during times of pain. Nothing will open the heavens *more*. Nothing!" (Russell M. Nelson, "Rejoice in the Gift of Priesthood Keys," *Liahona*, May 2024, 122).

42. See Russell M. Nelson, "The Everlasting Covenant," 5.

43. See Russell M. Nelson, "The Answer Is Always Jesus Christ," 127; see also endnote 14 in this message.

44. D. Todd Christofferson, "The Divine Gift of Repentance," *Ensign* or *Liahona*, Nov. 2011, 39.

45. Moses 5:11.

46. See 2 Nephi 2:26–28.

THE MAN WHO COMMUNED WITH JEHOVAH

ELDER KYLE S. MCKAY
Of the Seventy

My purpose this day and always is to testify of Jesus Christ, that He is the Son of God, the Creator and Savior of the world, our Deliverer and Redeemer. Because "the fundamental principles of our religion are the testimony of the Apostles and Prophets, concerning Jesus Christ,"[1] today I share with you my knowledge and testimony of the Savior as they have been strengthened and deepened by the life and teachings of one key apostle and prophet.

The Beginning of Wisdom

On the morning of a beautiful clear day early in the spring of 1820, 14-year-old Joseph Smith entered a grove of trees near his family's home to pray about his sins and to ask which church to join. His sincere prayer, offered with unwavering faith, received the attention of the most powerful forces in the universe, including the Father and the Son. And the devil. Each of these had an intense interest in that prayer and in that boy.

What we now call the First Vision marked the beginning of the Restoration of all things in this last dispensation. But for Joseph, the experience was also personal and preparatory. All he wanted was forgiveness and direction. The Lord gave him both. The instruction to "join none of [the churches]"[2] was directive. The words "Thy sins are forgiven thee"[3] were redemptive.

For all the beautiful truths we might learn from that First Vision, perhaps Joseph's main takeaway was simply, "I had found the testimony of James to be true—that a man who lacked wisdom might ask of God, and obtain."[4]

As one scholar noted: "The real resonance of the First Vision today is to know that it's the nature of God to give to those who lack wisdom. . . . The God that reveals Himself to Joseph Smith in the sacred grove is a God who answers teenagers in times of trouble."[5]

Joseph's experience in the grove gave him confidence to ask for *forgiveness* and *direction* for the rest of his life. His experience has also given *me* confidence to ask for forgiveness and direction for the rest of my life.

Regular Repentance

On September 21, 1823, Joseph earnestly prayed for forgiveness, confident that because of his experience in the grove three years earlier, heaven would respond again.[6] And it did. The Lord sent an angel, Moroni, to instruct Joseph and inform him of an ancient record he would later translate by the gift and power of God—the Book of Mormon.

Almost 13 years after that, Joseph and Oliver Cowdery knelt in solemn, silent prayer in the newly dedicated Kirtland Temple. We do not know what they prayed for, but their prayers likely included a plea for forgiveness, for, as they arose, the Savior appeared and declared, "Behold, your sins are forgiven you; you are clean before me."[7]

In the months and years after this experience, Joseph and Oliver would sin again. And again. But in that moment, *for* that moment, in response to their plea and in preparation for the glorious restoration of priesthood keys that was about to happen, Jesus made them sinless.

Joseph's life of regular repentance gives me confidence to "come boldly unto the throne of grace, that [I] may obtain mercy."[8] I have learned that Jesus Christ truly is "of a forgiving disposition."[9] It is neither His mission nor His nature to condemn. He came to save.[10]

Inquiring of the Lord

As part of the promised "restitution of all things," the Lord, through Joseph Smith, brought forth the Book of Mormon and other revelations that contain the fulness of His gospel. Vital truths were given clarity and completeness as Joseph repeatedly inquired of the Lord for direction. Consider the following:

1. The Father and the Son have bodies "as tangible as man's."[12]

2. Jesus took upon Himself not only our sins but also our sicknesses, afflictions, and infirmities.[13]

3. His Atonement was so excruciating it caused Him to bleed from every pore.[14]

4. We are saved by His grace "after all we can do."[15]

5. There are conditions to Christ's mercy.[16]

6. As we come unto Christ, He will not only forgive our sins, but He will also change our very nature so "that we have no more disposition to do evil."[17]

7. Christ always commands His people to build temples,[18] where He manifests Himself unto them[19] and endows them with power from on high.[20]

I testify that all these things are true and necessary. They represent only a fraction of the fulness that was restored by Jesus Christ through Joseph Smith in response to Joseph's recurring requests for direction.

Rolling on This Kingdom

In 1842, Joseph wrote of amazing things that would come to pass in this last dispensation. He declared that during our day, "the heavenly Priesthood will unite with the earthly, to bring about those great purposes; and whilst we are thus united in the one common cause, to roll forth the kingdom of God, the heavenly Priesthood are not idle spectators."[21]

To his friend Benjamin Johnson, Joseph said, "Benjamin, [if I die] I [would] not be far away from you, and if on the other side of the veil, I [would] still be working with you, and with a power greatly increased, to roll on this kingdom."[22]

On June 27, 1844, Joseph Smith and his brother Hyrum were murdered. Joseph's body was laid to rest, but his testimony continues to reverberate around the world and in my soul:

"I had seen a vision; I knew it, and I knew that God knew it, and I could not deny it."[23]

"I never told you I was perfect; but there is no error in the revelations which I have taught."[24]

"The fundamental principles of our religion are the testimony of the Apostles and Prophets, concerning Jesus Christ, that He died, was buried, and rose again the third day, and ascended into heaven; and all other things which pertain to our religion are only appendages to it."[25]

What was said of John the Baptist might also be said of Joseph Smith: "There was a man sent from God, whose name was [Joseph]. . . . He was not that Light, but was sent to bear witness of that Light," "that all men through him might believe."[26]

I believe. I believe and am sure that Jesus is the Christ, the Son of the living God. I testify that the living God is our loving Father. I know this because the voice of the Lord has spoken it to me, and so has the voice of His servants, the apostles and prophets, including and beginning with Joseph Smith.

I testify that Joseph Smith was and is a prophet of God, a witness and servant of the Lord Jesus Christ. He was "blessed to open the last dispensation,"[27] and we are blessed that he did.

The Lord commanded Oliver and all of us, "Stand by my servant Joseph, faithfully."[28] I testify that the Lord stands by His servant Joseph and the Restoration wrought through him.

Joseph Smith is now part of that heavenly priesthood of which he spoke. As he promised his friend, he is not far away from us, and on the other side of the veil, he is still working with us, and with a power greatly increased, to roll on this kingdom. With joy and thanksgiving, I raise my voice in "praise to the man who communed with Jehovah."[29] And above all, praise to Jehovah, who communed with that man! In the name of Jesus Christ, amen.

Notes

1. *Teachings of Presidents of the Church: Joseph Smith* (2007), 49.
2. Joseph Smith—History 1:19.
3. Joseph Smith, History, circa summer 1832, 3, josephsmithpapers.org.
4. Joseph Smith—History 1:26.
5. Steven Harper, in Spencer W. McBride, host, *The Fist Vision: A Joseph Smith Papers Project*, podcast, episode 6, "I Had Seen a Vision," Joseph Smith Papers Project, May 16, 2024, ChurchofJesusChrist.org.
6. See Joseph Smith—History 1:28–29.
7. Doctrine and Covenants 110:5.
8. Hebrews 4:16.

9. *Lectures on Faith* (1985), 42.
10. See John 3:17; 8:3–11.
11. Acts 3:21.
12. Doctrine and Covenants 130:22.
13. See Alma 7:11–12.
14. See Doctrine and Covenants 19:18.
15. 2 Nephi 25:23.
16. See Mosiah 4:8; Alma 42:13, 23–24.
17. Mosiah 5:2.
18. See Doctrine and Covenants 124:39.
19. See Doctrine and Covenants 109:5; 110:7–8.
20. See Doctrine and Covenants 43:16; 109:22.
21. *Teachings: Joseph Smith*, 514.
22. Joseph Smith, in Benjamin F. Johnson letter to George S. Gibbs, circa 1903, Church History Library, Salt Lake City.
23. Joseph Smith—History 1:25.
24. *Teachings: Joseph Smith*, 522.
25. *Teachings: Joseph Smith*, 49.
26. John 1:6, 8, 7.
27. "Praise to the Man," *Hymns*, no. 27.
28. Doctrine and Covenants 6:18.
29. *Hymns*, no. 27.

EMBRACE THE LORD'S GIFT OF REPENTANCE

ELDER JORGE M. ALVARADO
Of the Seventy

I testify of a loving Heavenly Father. In the April 2019 general conference, moments after I was sustained in my new responsibility as a General Authority Seventy, the choir sang a rendition of "I Stand All Amazed" that pierced my heart and soul.

> *I marvel that he would descend from his throne divine*
> *To rescue a soul so rebellious and proud as mine,*
> *That he should extend his great love unto such as I,*
> *Sufficient to own, to redeem, and to justify.*[1]

As I heard those words, I was all amazed. I felt that despite my inadequacies and flaws, the Lord blessed me to know that "in his strength I can do all things."[2]

The common feeling of inadequacy, weakness, or even unworthiness is something with which many of us sometimes struggle. I still struggle with this; I felt it the day I was called. I have felt it many times, and I still feel it right now speaking to you. However, I have learned that I am not alone with these feelings. In fact, there are many accounts in the scriptures of those who seem to have felt similar feelings. For example, we remember Nephi as a faithful and valiant servant of the Lord. At times, even he struggled with feelings of unworthiness, weakness, and inadequacy.

He said: "Notwithstanding the great goodness of the Lord, in showing me his great and marvelous works, my heart exclaimeth: O wretched man that I am! Yea, my heart sorroweth because of my flesh; my soul grieveth because of mine iniquities."[3]

The Prophet Joseph Smith spoke of often feeling "condemned," in his youth, "for [his] weakness and imperfections."[4] But Joseph's feelings of inadequacy and worry were part of what led him to ponder, study, learn, and pray. As you may remember, he went to pray in the grove near his home to find truth, peace, and forgiveness. He heard the Lord say: "Joseph, my son, thy sins are forgiven thee. Go thy way, walk in my statutes, and keep my commandments. Behold, I am the Lord of Glory. I was crucified for the world that all those who believe on my name may have eternal life."[5]

Joseph's sincere desire to repent and seek the salvation of his soul helped him come to Jesus Christ and receive forgiveness of his sins. This continuous effort opened the door to the continuing Restoration of the gospel of Jesus Christ.

This remarkable experience of the Prophet Joseph Smith illustrates how feelings of weakness and inadequacy can help us recognize our fallen nature. If we are humble, this will help us come to recognize our dependence upon Jesus Christ and stir within our hearts a sincere desire to turn to the Savior and repent of our sins.[6]

My friends, repentance is joy![7] Sweet repentance is part of a daily process through which, "line upon line, precept upon precept,"[8] the Lord teaches us to live a life centered in His teachings. Like Joseph and Nephi, we can "cry unto [God] for mercy; for he is mighty to save."[9] He can fulfill any righteous desire or longing and can heal any wound in our lives.

In the Book of Mormon: Another Testament of Jesus Christ, you and I can find countless accounts of individuals who learned how to come unto Christ through sincere repentance.

I'd like to share with you an example of the tender mercies of the Lord through an experience that occurred in my beloved home island of Puerto Rico.

It was in my hometown of Ponce that a sister in the Church, Célia Cruz Ayala, decided that she was going to give a Book of Mormon to a friend. She wrapped it and went to deliver this gift, more precious to her than diamonds or rubies, she said.[10] On her way, a thief approached her, grabbed her purse, and ran away with the special gift inside.

When she told this story at church, her friend said, "Who knows? Maybe this was your opportunity to share the gospel!"

Well, a few days later, do you know what happened? Célia

received a letter. I hold that letter, which Célia shared with me, in my hand today. It says:

"Mrs. Cruz:

"Forgive me, forgive me. You will never know how sorry I am for attacking you. But because of it, my life has changed and will continue to change.

"That book [the Book of Mormon] has helped me in my life. The dream of that man of God has shaken me. . . . I am returning your five [dollars,] for I can't spend them. I want you to know that you seemed to have a radiance about you. That light seemed to stop me [from harming you, so] I ran away instead.

"I want you to know that you will see me again, but when you do, you won't recognize me, for I will be your brother. . . . Here, where I live, I have to find the Lord and go to the church you belong to.

"The message you wrote in that book brought tears to my eyes. Since Wednesday night I have not been able to stop reading it. I have prayed and asked God to forgive me [and] I ask you to forgive me. . . . I thought your wrapped gift was something I could sell. [Instead,] it has made me want to [change] my life. . . . Forgive me, forgive me, I beg you.

"Your absent friend."[11]

Brothers and sisters, the light of the Savior can reach us all, no matter our circumstances. "It is not possible for you to sink lower than the infinite light of Christ's Atonement shines," said President Jeffrey R. Holland.[12]

As for the unintended recipient of Célia's gift, the Book of Mormon, this brother went on to witness more of the Lord's mercy. Although it took time for this brother to forgive himself, he found joy in repentance. What a miracle! One faithful sister, one Book of Mormon, sincere repentance, and the Savior's power led to the enjoyment of the fulness of blessings of the gospel and sacred covenants in the house of the Lord.[13] Other family members followed and accepted sacred responsibilities in the Lord's vineyard, including full-time missionary service.[14]

As we come unto Jesus Christ, our path of sincere repentance will eventually lead us to the Savior's holy temple.

What a righteous motive to strive to be clean—to be worthy of the fulness of the blessings made possible by our Heavenly Father and His Son through sacred temple covenants! Serving regularly in the house of the Lord and striving to keep the sacred covenants we make there will increase both our desire and our ability to experience the change of heart, might, mind, and soul necessary for us to become more like our Savior. President Russell M. Nelson has testified: "Nothing will open the heavens *more* [than worshipping in the temple]. Nothing!"[15]

My dear friends, do you feel inadequate? Do you feel unworthy? Are you second-guessing yourself? Perhaps you might worry and ask: Do I measure up? Is it too late for me? Why do I keep failing when I am trying my absolute best?[16]

Brothers and sisters, surely we will make mistakes in our lives along the way. But please remember that, as Elder Gerrit W. Gong has taught: "Our Savior's Atonement is infinite and eternal. Each of us strays and falls short. We may, for a time, lose our way. God lovingly assures us [that] no matter where we are or what we have done, there is no point of no return. He waits ready to embrace us."[17]

As my dear wife, Cari Lu, has also taught me, we all need to repent, rewind, and reset the time to "zero o'clock" every single day.

Obstacles will come. Let us not wait for things to get hard before turning to God. Let us not wait until the end of our mortal lives to truly repent. Instead, let us now, no matter which part of the covenant path we are on, focus on the redemptive power of Jesus Christ and on Heavenly Father's desire for us to return to Him.[18]

The Lord's house, His holy scriptures, His holy prophets and apostles inspire us to strive towards personal holiness through the doctrine of Christ.[19]

And Nephi said: "And now, behold, my beloved brethren, this is the way; and there is none other way nor name given under heaven whereby man [and woman] can be saved in the kingdom of God. And now, behold, this is the doctrine of Christ, and the only and true doctrine of the Father, and of the Son, and of the Holy Ghost."[20]

Our process of "at-one-ment" with God may feel challenging. But you and I can pause, be still, look to the Savior, and seek to find and act on what He would have us change. If we do so with full intent, we will witness His healing. And think of how our posterity will be blessed as we embrace the Lord's gift of repentance![21]

The Master Potter, taught my dad, will mold and refine us, which can be difficult. Nonetheless, the Master Healer will also cleanse us. I have experienced and continue to experience that healing power. I testify that it comes through faith in Jesus Christ and daily repentance.

> *Oh, it is wonderful that he should care for me*
> *Enough to die for me!*[22]

I testify of God's love and of the infinite power of His Son's Atonement. We can feel it profoundly as we sincerely and wholeheartedly repent.

My friends, I am a witness of the glorious Restoration of the gospel through the Prophet Joseph Smith and the current divine guidance of the Savior through His prophet and mouthpiece, President Russell M. Nelson. I know Jesus Christ lives and that He is the Master Healer of our souls. I know and I testify that these things are true, in the holy name of Jesus Christ, amen.

Notes

1. "I Stand All Amazed," *Hymns*, no. 193.
2. Alma 26:12.
3. 2 Nephi 4:17; see also verses 18–19.
4. Joseph Smith—History 1:29.
5. Joseph Smith, "History, circa Summer 1832," 3, josephsmithpapers.org; spelling and punctuation standardized.
6. See Mosiah 4:11–12.
7. President Russell M. Nelson taught: "When we choose to repent, we choose to change! We allow the Savior to transform us into the best version of ourselves. We choose to grow spiritually and receive joy—the joy of redemption in Him. When we choose to repent, we choose to become more like Jesus Christ!" ("We Can Do Better and Be Better," *Ensign* or *Liahona*, May 2019, 67).
8. 2 Nephi 28:30.
9. Alma 34:18.
10. "My brothers and sisters, how precious *is* the Book of Mormon to you? If you were offered

diamonds or rubies *or* the Book of Mormon, which would you choose? Honestly, which *is* of greater worth to you?" (Russell M. Nelson, "The Book of Mormon: What Would Your Life Be Like without It?," *Ensign* or *Liahona*, Nov. 2017, 61).

11. In F. Burton Howard, "Missionary Moments: 'My Life Has Changed,'" *Church News*, Jan. 6, 1996, thechurchnews.com; see also *Saints: The Story of the Church of Jesus Christ in the Latter Days*, vol. 4, *Sounded in Every Ear*, 1955–2020 (2024), 472–74, 477–79.
12. Jeffrey R. Holland, "The Laborers in the Vineyard," *Ensign* or *Liahona*, May 2012, 33.
13. May we stop for one second and think about our posterity? Because of our myopic view, we cannot see it now, but our willingness to turn to the Lord with full purpose of heart—to change, repent, and embrace the gospel of Jesus Christ—can influence generations! Imagine the additional blessings that may blossom from one soul's humility, meekness, and faith in Jesus Christ under even the most inconvenient of circumstances!
14. These details were recounted by Sister Célia Cruz in a personal conversation with Elder Jorge M. Alvarado on September 10, 2024.
15. Russell M. Nelson, "Rejoice in the Gift of Priesthood Keys," *Liahona*, May 2024, 122.
16. When we find ourselves asking questions like these, it is important to remember the words of the Apostle Paul:

     "Who shall separate us from the love of Christ? shall tribulation, or distress, or persecution, or famine, or nakedness, or peril, or sword? . . .

     "Nay, in all these things we are more than conquerors through him that loved us.

     "For I am persuaded, that neither death, nor life, nor angels, nor principalities, nor powers, nor things present, nor things to come,

     "Nor height, nor depth, nor any other creature, shall be able to separate us from the love of God, which is in Christ Jesus our Lord" (Romans 8:35, 37–39).
17. Gerrit W. Gong, "Our Campfire of Faith," *Ensign* or *Liahona*, Nov. 2018, 41.
18. Nephi is a good example of this. He exclaimed:

     "Awake, my soul! No longer droop in sin. Rejoice, O my heart, and give place no more for the enemy of my soul. . . .

     "O Lord, wilt thou redeem my soul? Wilt thou deliver me out of the hands of mine enemies? Wilt thou make me that I may shake at the appearance of sin?" (2 Nephi 4:28, 31).
19. President Dallin H. Oaks taught: "When a person has gone through the [repentance] process . . . , the Savior does more than cleanse that person from sin. He also gives him or her new strength. That strengthening is essential for us to realize the purpose of the cleansing, which is to return to our Heavenly Father. To be admitted to His presence, we must be more than clean. We must also be changed from a morally weak person who has sinned into a strong person with the spiritual stature to dwell in the presence of God" ("The Atonement and Faith," *Ensign*, Apr. 2010, 33–34).
20. 2 Nephi 31:21.
21. We honor our family and Heavenly Father by embracing repentance and striving to live a good life.
22. *Hymns*, no. 193.

IN THE SPACE OF NOT MANY YEARS

ELDER DAVID A. BEDNAR
Of the Quorum of the Twelve Apostles

My beloved brothers and sisters, sitting on the stand today, I have watched this Conference Center fill up three times, for the first time since COVID. You are devoted disciples of Jesus Christ who are eager to learn. I commend you for your faithfulness. And I love you.

Ezra Taft Benson served as the President of The Church of Jesus Christ of Latter-day Saints from November 1985 until May 1994. I was 33 years old when President Benson became the President of the Church and 42 when he passed away. And his teachings and testimony influenced me in profound and powerful ways.

One of the hallmarks of President Benson's ministry was his focus upon the purpose and importance of the Book of Mormon. He emphasized repeatedly that "the Book of Mormon is the keystone of our religion—the keystone of our testimony, the keystone of our doctrine, and the keystone in the witness of our Lord and Savior."[1] He also often emphasized teachings and warnings about the sin of pride found in this latter-day testament of Jesus Christ.

A particular teaching by President Benson greatly impacted me and continues to influence my study of the Book of Mormon. He said:

"The Book of Mormon . . . was written for our day. The Nephites never had the book; neither did the Lamanites of ancient times. It was meant for us. Mormon wrote near the end of the Nephite civilization. Under the inspiration of God, who sees all things from the beginning, [Mormon] abridged centuries of records, choosing the stories, speeches, and events that would be most helpful to us."[2]

President Benson continued: "Each of the major writers of the Book of Mormon testified that he wrote for future generations. . . . If they saw our day, and chose those things which would be of greatest worth to us, is not that how we should study the Book of

107

Mormon? We should constantly ask ourselves, 'Why did the Lord inspire Mormon . . . to include [this account] in his record? What lesson can I learn from [this admonition] to help me live in this day and age?'"

President Benson's statements help us to understand that the Book of Mormon is not primarily a historical record that looks to the past. Rather, this volume of scripture looks to the future and contains important principles, warnings, and lessons intended for the circumstances and challenges of our day. Hence, the Book of Mormon is a book about our future and the times in which we do now and will yet live.

I pray for the assistance of the Holy Ghost as we now consider relevant lessons for us today from the book of Helaman in the Book of Mormon.

The Nephites and the Lamanites

The record of Helaman and his sons describes a people who were anticipating the birth of Jesus Christ. The half century recounted in the scriptural record highlights the conversion and righteousness of the Lamanites and the wickedness, apostasy, and abominations of the Nephites.

A series of comparisons and contrasts between the Nephites and Lamanites from this ancient record are most instructive for us today.

"The Lamanites had become, the more part of them, a righteous people, insomuch that their righteousness did exceed that of the Nephites, because of their firmness and their steadiness in the faith.

"[And] there were many of the Nephites who had become hardened and impenitent and grossly wicked, insomuch that they did reject the word of God and all the preaching and prophesying which did come among them."[3]

"And thus we see that the Nephites did begin to dwindle in unbelief, and grow in wickedness and abominations, while the Lamanites began to grow exceedingly in the knowledge of their God; yea, they did begin to keep his statutes and commandments, and to walk in truth and uprightness before him.

"And thus we see that the Spirit of the Lord began to withdraw from the Nephites, because of the wickedness and the hardness of their hearts.

"And thus we see that the Lord began to pour out his Spirit upon the Lamanites, because of their easiness and willingness to believe in his words."[4]

Perhaps the most stunning and sobering aspect of this decline into apostasy by the Nephites is the fact that "all these iniquities did come unto them in the space of not many years."[5]

The Nephites Turned Away from God

How could a once-righteous people become hardened and wicked in such a short period of time? How could people so quickly forget the God who had blessed them so abundantly?

In a powerful and profound way, the negative example of the Nephites is instructive for us today.

"Pride . . . began to enter . . . into the hearts of the people who professed to belong to the church of God . . . because of their exceedingly great riches and their prosperity in the land."[6]

"[They] set [their] hearts upon the riches and the vain things of this world"[7] "because of that pride which [they] . . . suffered to enter [into their] hearts, which . . . lifted [them] up beyond that which is good because of [their] exceedingly great riches!"[8]

Ancient voices from the dust plead with us today to learn this everlasting lesson: prosperity, possessions, and ease[9] constitute a potent mixture that can lead even the righteous to drink the spiritual poison of pride.

Allowing pride to enter into our hearts can cause us to mock that which is sacred;[10] disbelieve in the spirit of prophecy and revelation;[11] trample under our feet the commandments of God;[12] deny the word of God;[13] cast out, mock,[14] and revile against the prophets;[15] and forget the Lord our God[16] and "not desire that the Lord [our] God, who hath created [us], should rule and reign over [us]."[17]

Therefore, if we are not faithful and obedient, we can transform the God-given blessing of prosperity into a prideful curse that diverts and distracts us from eternal truths and vital spiritual priorities. We always must be on guard against a pride-induced and exaggerated sense of self-importance, a misguided evaluation of our own self-sufficiency, and seeking self instead of serving others.

As we pridefully focus upon ourselves, we also are afflicted with spiritual blindness and miss much, most, or perhaps all that is occurring within and around us. We cannot look to and focus upon Jesus Christ as the "mark"[18] if we only see ourselves.

Such spiritual blindness also can cause us to turn out of the way of righteousness,[19] fall away into forbidden paths, and become lost.[20] As we blindly "turn unto [our] own ways"[21] and follow destructive detours, we are inclined to lean upon our own understanding,[22] boast in our own strength,[23] and depend upon our own wisdom.[24]

Samuel the Lamanite succinctly summarized the turning away from God by the Nephites: "Ye have sought all the days of your lives for that which ye could not obtain; and ye have sought for happiness in doing iniquity, which thing is contrary to the nature of that righteousness which is in our great and Eternal Head."[25]

The prophet Mormon observed, "The more part of the people [remained] in their pride and wickedness, and the lesser part [walked] more circumspectly before God."[26]

The Lamanites Turned to God

In the Book of Helaman, the increasing righteousness of the Lamanites provides a stark contrast to the rapid spiritual decline of the Nephites.

The Lamanites turned to God and were brought to a knowledge of the truth by believing the teachings in the holy scriptures and of prophets, exercising faith in the Lord Jesus Christ, repenting of their sins, and experiencing a mighty change of heart.[27]

"Therefore, as many as have come to this, ye know of yourselves are firm and steadfast in the faith, and in the thing wherewith they have been made free."[28]

"Ye should behold that the more part of [the Lamanites] are in the path of their duty, and they do walk circumspectly before God, and they do observe to keep his commandments and his statutes and his judgments. . . .

" . . . They are striving with unwearied diligence that they may bring the remainder of their brethren to the knowledge of the truth."[29]

As a consequence, the "righteousness [of the Lamanites] did exceed that of the Nephites, because of their firmness and their steadiness in the faith."[30]

A Warning and a Promise

Moroni declared: "Behold, the Lord hath shown unto me great and marvelous things concerning that which must shortly come, at that day when these things shall come forth among you.

"Behold, I speak unto you as if ye were present, and yet ye are not. But behold, Jesus Christ hath shown you unto me, and I know your doing."[31]

Please remember that the Book of Mormon looks to the future and contains important principles, warnings, and lessons intended for me and you in the circumstances and challenges of our present day.

Apostasy can occur at two basic levels—institutional and individual. At the institutional level, The Church of Jesus Christ of Latter-day Saints will not be lost through apostasy or taken from the earth.

The Prophet Joseph Smith proclaimed: "The Standard of Truth has been erected; no unhallowed hand can stop the work from progressing . . . ; the truth of God will go forth boldly, nobly, and independent, till it has penetrated every continent, visited every clime, swept every country, and sounded in every ear, till the purposes of God shall be accomplished, and the Great Jehovah shall say the work is done."[32]

At the individual level, each of us must "beware of pride, lest [we] become as the Nephites of old."[33]

May I suggest that if you or I believe we are sufficiently strong and stalwart to avoid the arrogance of pride, then perhaps we already are suffering from this deadly spiritual disease. Simply stated, if you or I do not believe we could be afflicted with and by pride, then we are vulnerable and in spiritual danger. In the space of not many days, weeks, months, or years, we might forfeit our spiritual birthright for far less than a mess of pottage.[34]

If, however, you or I believe we could be afflicted with and by pride, then we consistently will do the small and simple things[35] that will protect and help us become "as a child, submissive, meek, humble, patient, full of love, willing to submit to all things which the Lord seeth fit to inflict upon [us]."[36] "Blessed are they who humble themselves without being compelled to be humble."[37]

As we follow President Benson's counsel and ask ourselves why the Lord inspired Mormon to include in his abridgment of the book of Helaman the accounts, admonitions, and warnings that he did, I promise we will discern the applicability of these teachings to the specific conditions of our individual lives and families today. As we study and ponder this inspired record, we will be blessed with eyes to see, ears to hear, minds to comprehend, and hearts to understand[38] the lessons we should learn to "beware of pride, lest [we should] enter into temptation."[39]

I joyfully witness that God the Eternal Father is our Father. Jesus Christ is His Only Begotten and Beloved Son. He is our Savior. And I testify that as we walk in the meekness of the Lord's Spirit, we will avoid and overcome pride and have peace in Him.[40] I so witness in the sacred name of the Lord Jesus Christ, amen.

Notes

1. Ezra Taft Benson, "The Book of Mormon—Keystone of Our Religion," *Ensign*, Nov. 1986, 6.
2. Ezra Taft Benson, "The Book of Mormon—Keystone of Our Religion," 6.
3. Helaman 6:1–2.
4. Helaman 6:34–36.
5. Helaman 6:32.
6. Helaman 3:33, 36.
7. Helaman 7:21.
8. Helaman 7:26.
9. See Helaman 12:2.
10. See Helaman 4:12.
11. See Helaman 4:23.
12. See Helaman 6:31.
13. See Helaman 8:13.
14. See Helaman 13:24.
15. See Helaman 10:15.

16. See Helaman 12:2.
17. Helaman 12:6.
18. See Jacob 4:14.
19. See Helaman 6:31.
20. See 1 Nephi 8:28.
21. Helaman 6:31.
22. See Proverbs 3:5.
23. See Helaman 4:13.
24. See Helaman 16:15.
25. Helaman 13:38.
26. Helaman 16:10.
27. See Helaman 15:7.
28. Helaman 15:8.
29. Helaman 15:5–6.
30. Helaman 6:1.
31. Mormon 8:34–35.
32. *Teachings of Presidents of the Church: Joseph Smith* (2007), 142.
33. Doctrine and Covenants 38:39.
34. See Genesis 25:29–34.
35. See 1 Nephi 16:29; Alma 37:6–7; Doctrine and Covenants 64:32–33.
36. Mosiah 3:19.
37. Alma 32:16.
38. See Mosiah 2:9.
39. Doctrine and Covenants 23:1.
40. See Doctrine and Covenants 19:23.

Sunday Morning Session

OCTOBER 6, 2024

"I AM HE"

PRESIDENT JEFFREY R. HOLLAND
Acting President of the Quorum of the Twelve Apostles

It is the Sabbath day, and we have gathered to speak of Christ and Him crucified. I know that my Redeemer lives.

Consider this scene from the last week of Jesus's mortal life. A multitude had gathered, including Roman soldiers armed with staves and strapped with swords. Led by officers from the chief priests who had torches in hand, this earnest company was *not* off to conquer a city.[1] Tonight they were looking for only one man, a man not known to carry a weapon, receive military training, or engage in physical combat at any time in His entire life.

As the soldiers approached, Jesus, in an effort to protect His disciples, stepped forth and said, "Whom seek ye?" They replied, "Jesus of Nazareth." Jesus said, "I am he. . . . As soon . . . as he had said unto them, I am he, they went backward, and fell to the ground."[2]

To me, that is one of the most stirring lines in all of scripture. Among other things, it tells me straightforwardly that *just being in the presence* of the Son of God—the great Jehovah of the Old Testament and Good Shepherd of the New, who bears no weapons of any kind—that *just hearing the voice* of this Refuge from the Storm, this Prince of Peace, is enough to send antagonists stumbling into retreat, piling them in a jumble, making the whole group wish they had been assigned kitchen duty that night.

Just a few days earlier, when He had entered the city triumphantly, "all the city was moved," the scripture says, asking, "Who is this?"[3] I can only imagine that "Who is this?" is the question those muddled soldiers were now asking!

The *answer* to that question could not have been in His looks, for Isaiah had prophesied some seven centuries earlier that "he hath no form nor comeliness; and when we shall see him, there is no beauty that we should desire him."[4] It certainly wasn't in His polished wardrobe or His great personal wealth, of which He had neither. It could not be from any professional training in the local synagogues because we have no evidence that He ever studied at any of them, though even in His youth He could confound superbly prepared scribes and lawyers, astonishing them with His doctrine "as one having authority."[5]

From that teaching in the temple to His triumphant entry into Jerusalem and this final, unjustifiable arrest, Jesus was routinely placed in difficult, often devious situations in which He was always triumphant—victories for which we have no explanation except divine DNA.

Yet down through history many have simplified, even trivialized our image of Him and His witness of who He was. They have reduced His righteousness to mere prudishness, His justice to mere anger, His mercy to mere permissiveness. We must not be guilty of such simplistic versions of Him that conveniently ignore teachings we find uncomfortable. This "dumbing down" has been true even regarding His ultimate defining virtue, His love.

During His mortal mission, Jesus taught that there were two great commandments. They have been taught in this conference and will forever be taught: "Love the Lord thy God [and] love thy neighbour as thyself."[6] If we are to follow the Savior faithfully in these two crucial and inextricably linked rules, we ought to hold firmly to what He *actually* said. And what He *actually* said was, "If ye love me, keep my commandments."[7] On that same evening, He said we were to "love one another; as I have loved you."[8]

In those scriptures, those qualifying phrases defining true, Christlike love—sometimes referred to as charity—are absolutely essential.

What do they define? How did Jesus love?

First, He loved with "all [of His] heart, might, mind and strength,"[9] giving Him the ability to heal the deepest pain and declare the hardest reality. In short, He is one who could administer grace and insist on truth at the same time.[10] As Lehi said in his blessing to his son Jacob, "Redemption cometh in and through the Holy Messiah; for he is full of grace and truth."[11] His love allows an encouraging embrace when it is needed and a bitter cup when it has to be swallowed. So we try to love—with all of our heart, might, mind, and strength—because that is the way He loves us.

The second characteristic of Jesus's divine charity was His obedience to *every word* that proceeded from God's mouth,[12] always aligning His will and behavior with that of His Heavenly Father.[13]

When He arrived on the Western Hemisphere following His Resurrection, Christ said to the Nephites: "Behold, I am Jesus Christ. . . . I have drunk out of that bitter cup which the Father hath given me, . . . in the which I have suffered the will of the Father . . . from the beginning."[14]

Of the myriad ways He could have introduced Himself, Jesus did so *by declaring His obedience to the will of the Father*—never mind that not long before in His hour of greatest need, this Only Begotten Son of God had felt totally abandoned by His Father.[15] Christ's charity—*evident in complete loyalty to divine will*—persisted and continues to persist, not just through the easy and comfortable days but especially through the darkest and most difficult ones.

Jesus was "a man of sorrows,"[16] the scriptures say. He experienced sadness, fatigue, disappointment, and excruciating loneliness. In these and in all times, Jesus's love faileth not, and neither does His Father's. With such mature love—the kind that exemplifies, empowers, and imparts—ours will not fail either.

So, if sometimes the harder you try, the more difficult it seems to get; if, just as you try to work on your limitations and your shortcomings, you find someone or something determined to challenge your faith; if, as you labor devotedly, you still feel moments of fear wash over you, remember that it has been so for some of the most faithful and marvelous people in every era of time. Also remember that there is a force in the universe determined to oppose *every good thing* you try to do.[17]

So, through abundance as well as poverty, through private acclaim as well as public criticism, through the divine elements of the Restoration as well as the human foibles that will inevitably be part of it, *we stay the course with* the true Church of Christ. Why? Because as with our Redeemer, we signed on for the whole term—not ending with the first short introductory quiz but through to the final exam. The joy in this is that the Headmaster gave us all open-book answers *before the course began*. Furthermore, we have a host of tutors who remind us of these answers at regular stops along the way. But of course, none of this works if we keep cutting class.

"Whom seek ye?" With all our hearts we answer, "Jesus of Nazareth." When He says, "I am he,"[18] we bow our knee and confess with our tongue that He is the living Christ, that He alone atoned for our sins, that He was carrying us even when we thought He had abandoned us. When we stand before Him and see the wounds in His hands and feet, we will begin to comprehend what it meant for Him *to bear our sins and be acquainted with grief, to be completely obedient to the will of His Father*—all out of pure love for us. To introduce others to faith, repentance, baptism, the gift of the Holy Ghost, and receiving our blessings in the house of the Lord—these are the fundamental "principles and ordinances"[19] that ultimately reveal our love of God and neighbor and joyfully characterize the true Church of Christ.

Brothers and sisters, I testify that The Church of Jesus Christ of Latter-day Saints is the vehicle God has provided for our exaltation. The gospel it teaches is true, and the priesthood legitimizing it is not derivative. I testify that Russell M. Nelson is a prophet of our God, as His predecessors were and as His successors will be. And one day that prophetic guidance will lead a generation to see our Messenger of Salvation descend like "lightning . . . out of the east,"[20] and we will exclaim, "Jesus of Nazareth." With arms forever outstretched and love unfeigned, He will reply, "I am he."[21] I so promise with the apostolic power and authority of His holy name, even Jesus Christ, amen.

Notes

1. See Matthew 26:47–57; Mark 14:43–46.
2. John 18:4–6.
3. Matthew 21:10.
4. Isaiah 53:2.
5. Matthew 7:29; see also John 7:15.
6. Matthew 22:37, 39.
7. John 14:15.

8. John 13:34.
9. Doctrine and Covenants 4:2.
10. See Joseph Smith Translation, John 1:4, 14; Moses 1:6.
11. 2 Nephi 2:6.
12. See Doctrine and Covenants 84:44.
13. See Mosiah 15:7; 3 Nephi 27:13–15. And Jesus reminds us to do the same in Matthew 7:21: "Not every one that saith unto me, Lord, Lord, shall enter into the kingdom of heaven; but he that doeth the will of my Father which is in heaven."
14. 3 Nephi 11:10–11.
15. See Matthew 27:46.
16. Isaiah 53:3.
17. See Moroni 7:12.
18. John 18:4–6.
19. Articles of Faith 1:4.
20. Matthew 24:27.
21. John 18:5.

SEEKING ANSWERS TO SPIRITUAL QUESTIONS

SISTER TRACY Y. BROWNING

Second Counselor in the Primary General Presidency

I know this may come as a surprise, but I'm old enough to remember when we were taught in school that there were nine planets in our solar system. One of those planets, Pluto, was given its name by 11-year-old Venetia Burney of Oxford, England, after its discovery in 1930.[1] And up until 1992, Pluto was believed to be the most distant object in our solar system. During this time, it was common to find childhood papier mâché models of our planetary neighborhood in classrooms and science fairs, each one illustrating Pluto's position on the known border. Many scientists believed that beyond that edge, the outer solar system consisted of empty space.[2]

However, a lingering question remained within the scientific community regarding the origin of a particular type of comet that astronomers regularly tracked.[3] And that question persisted for decades before the discovery of another distant region of our solar system. With the limited knowledge they had, scientists used those intervening decades to produce significant technological advances that allowed for further study and exploration. Their eventual breakthrough reconfigured our planetary zone and resulted in Pluto being rehomed to this new region of space and our solar system consisting of eight planets.

One leading planetary scientist and principal investigator for the New Horizons space mission tasked with exploring Pluto up close had this to say about this experience: "We thought we understood the geography of our solar system. We didn't. We thought we understood the population of planets in our solar system. And we were wrong."[4]

What is striking to me about this period of space exploration history are some parallels and key distinctions between the metaphorical pursuit of expanding scientific horizons and the journey that we, as children of God, undertake to seek answers to our spiritual questions. Specifically, how we can respond to the limits of our spiritual understanding and prepare ourselves for the next stage of personal growth—and where we can turn for help.

Line upon Line

Asking questions and searching for meaning are a natural and normal part of our mortal experience. At times, not readily having complete answers can bring us to the edge of our understanding, and those limitations can feel frustrating or overwhelming. Wondrously, Heavenly Father's plan of happiness for all of us is designed to help us progress despite our limitations and accomplish what we cannot accomplish on our own, *even without a complete knowledge of all things.* God's plan is merciful toward the limitations of our humanity; provides us with our Savior, Jesus Christ, to be our Good Shepherd; and inspires us to use our agency to choose Him.

Elder Dieter F. Uchtdorf has taught that "asking questions isn't a sign of weakness," but rather "it's a precursor of growth."[5] Speaking directly to our personal effort as seekers of truth, our prophet, President Russell M. Nelson, has taught that we must have "a deep desire" and "ask with a sincere heart [and] real intent, having faith in [Jesus] Christ." He has further taught that "'real intent' means that one *really intends* to follow the divine direction given."[6]

Our personal effort to grow in wisdom may lead us to examine our questions, complex or otherwise, through the lens of cause and effect, seeking out and recognizing patterns and then forming narratives to give shape to our understanding and fill in perceived gaps in knowledge. When we consider our pursuit of spiritual knowledge, however, these thoughtful processes may be helpful at times but on their own can be incomplete as we look to discern things pertaining to Heavenly Father and our Savior, Jesus Christ, Their gospel, Their Church, and Their plan for all of us.

God the Father and His Son's way of imparting Their wisdom to us prioritizes inviting the power of the Holy Ghost to be our personal teacher as we center Jesus Christ in our lives and in our faithful seeking for Their answers and Their meaning. They invite us to discover truth through devoted time spent studying holy scripture and to seek for latter-day revealed truth for our day and our time, imparted by modern-day prophets and apostles. They entreat us to spend regular, worshipful time in the house of the Lord and to take to our knees in prayer "to access information from heaven."[7] Jesus's promise to those present to hear His Sermon on the Mount is as true for us in our day as it was during His earthly ministry: "Ask, and it shall be given you; seek, and ye shall find; knock, and it shall be opened unto you."[8] Our Savior assures that "your Father which is in heaven give[s] good things to them that ask him."[9]

The Lord's method of teaching is "line upon line, precept upon precept."[10] We may be required to "wait upon the Lord"[11] in the space between our current line of understanding and the next yet to be delivered. This sacred space can be a place where our greatest spiritual conditioning can occur—the site where we can "bear with patience"[12] our earnest seeking and renew our strength to continue to keep the sacred promises we have made to God through covenant.

Our covenant relationship with Heavenly Father and Jesus Christ signals our prevailing citizenship in God's kingdom. And our residency therein requires aligning our life to divine principles and putting in the effort to grow spiritually.

Obedience

One key principle taught throughout the Book of Mormon is when God's children choose to demonstrate obedience and keep their covenants, they receive continual spiritual guidance and direction. The Lord has told us that through our obedience and diligence, we may gain knowledge and intelligence.[13] God's laws and commandments are not designed to be an obstacle in our life but a powerful gateway to personal revelation and spiritual education. President Nelson has taught the crucial truth that "revelation from God is always compatible with His eternal law" and further that "it never contradicts His doctrine."[14] Your willing obedience to God's commands, despite not having a complete knowledge of His reasons, places you in the company of His prophets. Moses 5 teaches us about a particular interaction between Adam and an angel of the Lord.

After the Lord gave Adam and Eve "commandments, that they should worship the Lord their God, and should offer the firstlings of their flocks, for an offering unto the Lord," the scriptures say that "Adam was *obedient* unto the commandments of the Lord." We go on to read that "after many days an angel of the Lord appeared unto Adam, saying: Why dost thou offer sacrifices unto the Lord? And Adam said unto him: *I know not, save the Lord commanded me.*"[15]

Adam's obedience *preceded* his understanding and *prepared* him to receive the *sacred knowledge* that he was participating in a *sacred symbol* of the Atonement of Jesus Christ. Our humble obedience will, likewise, pave the way for our spiritual discernment of God's ways and His divine purpose for each of us. Reaching to elevate our obedience brings us closer to our Savior, Jesus Christ, because obedience to His laws and commandments is effectually reaching out to Him.

Additionally, our fidelity to the knowledge and wisdom we have *already inherited* through our faithful adherence to gospel principles and sacred covenants is crucial preparation for our readiness to receive and be stewards of communications from the Holy Spirit.

Heavenly Father and Jesus Christ are the source of all truth[16] and share Their wisdom liberally.[17] Also, understanding that we do not possess any personal knowledge independent of God[18] can help us know who to turn to and where to place our primary trust.

Profound Trust

The Old Testament account of Naaman, the military leader who was healed of leprosy by the prophet Elisha, is a particular favorite of mine. The story illustrates how the firm faith of a "little maid" altered the course of one man's life and, for all believers, revealed the reach of God's mercy to those who place their trust in Him and His prophet. Though nameless, this young girl also helped to push our understanding forward. And Naaman's belief on her testimony inspired him to take his petition for healing to God's chosen servant.

Naaman's response to the prophet Elisha's instructions to wash in the river Jordan was at first skeptical and indignant. But an invitation for him to be *obedient* to the prophet's counsel made way for his healing and his dramatic understanding that God was real.[19]

We may find that some of our spiritual petitions have reasonably discernible answers and may not create significant discomfort for us. Or, like Naaman, we may find that other needs are more challenging and may create difficult and complex feelings within us. Or, similar to the description of the astronomers' early conclusions about our solar system, in our search for *spiritual truth*, we may reach less accurate interpretations if we rely exclusively on our own limited understanding, a sorrowful and unintended consequence of which may lead us away from the covenant path. And moreover, some questions may persist until God, who "has all power" and "all wisdom, and all understanding," who "comprehendeth all things" in His mercy, provides enlightenment through our belief on His name.[20]

One significant caution from Naaman's account is that resisting obedience to God's laws and commandments may prolong or delay our growth. We are blessed to have Jesus Christ as our Master Healer. Our obedience to God's laws and commandments can open the way for our Savior to provide the understanding and healing He knows we need, according to His prescribed treatment plan for us.

Elder Richard G. Scott taught that "this life is an experience in profound trust—trust in Jesus Christ, trust in His teachings, trust in our capacity as led by the Holy Spirit to obey those teachings for happiness now and for a purposeful, supremely happy eternal existence. To trust means to obey willingly without knowing the end from the beginning (see Prov. 3:5–7). To produce fruit, your trust in the Lord must be more powerful and enduring than your confidence in your own personal feelings and experience."

Elder Scott continues: "To exercise faith is to trust that the Lord knows what He is doing with you and that He can accomplish it for your eternal good even though you cannot understand how He can possibly do it."[21]

Closing Testimony

Dear friends, I testify that our sincere gospel questions can provide Heavenly Father and Jesus Christ with opportunities to help us grow. My personal effort to seek answers from the Lord to my own spiritual questions—past and present—has allowed me to use the space between the lines of my understanding and God's to practice obedience to Him and fidelity to the spiritual knowledge that I currently possess.

I testify that placing your trust in Heavenly Father and in His prophets, whom He has sent, will help you to spiritually elevate and push you forward toward God's expanded horizon. Your vantage will change because you will change. God knows that the higher you are, the farther you can see. Our Savior invites you to make that climb. In the name of Jesus Christ, amen.

Notes

1. See "Pluto Facts," science.nasa.gov.
2. See "Kuiper Belt: In Depth," science.nasa.gov.
3. See "Kuiper Belt: In Depth," science.nasa.gov.
4. Alan Stern, in "Expanding the Horizons of Knowledge," *APPEL News*, Apr. 12, 2016, appel.nasa.gov.
5. Dieter F. Uchtdorf, "The Reflection in the Water" (Church Educational System fireside for young adults, Nov. 1, 2009), CESdevotionals.ChurchofJesusChrist.org.
6. Russell M. Nelson, "Ask, Seek, Knock," *Ensign* or *Liahona*, Nov. 2009, 81.
7. Russell M. Nelson, "Ask, Seek, Knock," 81.
8. Matthew 7:7.
9. Matthew 7:11.
10. 2 Nephi 28:30.
11. Isaiah 40:31.
12. Alma 26:27.
13. See Doctrine and Covenants 130:18–19.
14. Russell M. Nelson, "Ask, Seek, Knock," 83.
15. Moses 5:5–6; emphasis added.
16. See Doctrine and Covenants 93:21–28.
17. See James 1:5.
18. See Mosiah 4:9.
19. See 2 Kings 5:1–15.
20. Alma 26:35.
21. Richard G. Scott, "Trust in the Lord," *Ensign*, Nov. 1995, 17.

MORTALITY WORKS!

ELDER BROOK P. HALES
Of the Seventy

For several years I was assigned to home teach an older sister in my ward. She did not have an easy life. She had various health problems and experienced a lifetime of pain due to a childhood accident on the playground. Divorced at age 32 with four young children to raise and provide for, she remarried at age 50. Her second husband passed away when she was 66, and this sister lived an additional 26 years as a widow.

Despite her lifelong challenges, she was faithful to her covenants to the end. This sister was an avid genealogist, a temple attender, and a collector and writer of family histories. Though she had many difficult trials, and without question she felt at times sadness and loneliness, she had a cheerful countenance and a gracious and pleasant personality.

Nine months after her passing, one of her sons had a remarkable experience in the temple. He learned by the power of the Holy Ghost that his mother had a message for him. She communicated with him, but not by vision or audible words. The following unmistakable message came into the son's mind from his mother: "I want you to know that mortality works, and I want you to know that I now understand why everything happened [in my life] the way it did—and it is all OK."[1]

This message is all the more remarkable when one considers her situation and the difficulties this sister endured and overcame.

Brothers and sisters, mortality works! It is designed to work! Despite the challenges, heartaches, and difficulties we all face, our loving, wise, and perfect Heavenly Father has designed the plan of happiness such that we are not destined to fail. His plan provides a way for us to rise above our mortal failures. The Lord has said, "This is my work and my glory—to bring to pass the immortality and eternal life of man."[2]

Nonetheless, if we are to be the beneficiaries of the Lord's "work and . . . glory," even "immortality and eternal life," we must expect to be schooled and taught and to pass through the refiner's fire—sometimes to our utter limits. To completely avoid the problems, challenges, and difficulties of this world would be to sidestep the process that is truly necessary for mortality to work.

And so we should not be surprised when hard times come upon us. We will encounter situations that try us and people who enable us to practice true charity and patience. But we need to bear up under our difficulties and remember, as the Lord said:

"And whoso layeth down his life in my cause, for my name's sake, shall find it again, even life eternal.

"Therefore, be not afraid of your enemies [or your problems, challenges, or the tests of this life], for I have decreed . . . , saith the Lord, that I will prove you in all things, whether you will abide in my covenant . . . that you may be found worthy."[3]

When we feel distraught or anxious about our problems or feel that we might be receiving more than our fair share of life's difficulties, we can remember what the Lord said to the children of Israel:

"And thou shalt remember all the way[s] which the Lord thy God led thee these forty years in the wilderness, to humble thee, and to prove thee, to know what [is] in thine heart, whether thou [would] keep his commandments, or no."[4]

As Lehi taught his son Jacob:

"Thou hast suffered afflictions and much sorrow. . . . Nevertheless, . . . [God] shall consecrate thine afflictions for thy gain. . . . Wherefore, I know that thou art redeemed, because of the righteousness of thy Redeemer."[5]

Because this life is a testing ground and "dark clouds of trouble hang o'er us and threaten our peace to destroy,"[6] it is helpful to remember this counsel and promise found in Mosiah 23 relating to life's challenges: "Nevertheless—whosoever putteth his trust in [the Lord] the same shall be lifted up at the last day."[7]

As a youth, I personally experienced great emotional pain and shame that came as the result of the unrighteous actions of another, which for many years affected my self-worth and my sense of worthiness before the Lord. Nevertheless, I bear personal witness that the Lord can strengthen us and bear us up in whatever difficulties we are called upon to experience during our sojourn in this vale of tears.

We are familiar with Paul's experience:

"And lest I should be exalted above measure through the abundance of the revelations [I have received], there was given to me a thorn in the flesh, the messenger of Satan to buffet me, lest I should be exalted above measure.

"For this thing I besought the Lord thrice, that it might depart from me.

"And he said unto me, My grace is sufficient for thee: for my strength is made perfect in weakness. Most gladly therefore will I rather glory in my infirmities, that the power of Christ may rest upon me."[8]

We don't know what Paul's "thorn in the flesh" was. He chose not to describe whether it was a physical ailment, a mental or emotional infirmity, or a temptation. But we don't need to know that detail to know that he struggled and pleaded with the Lord for help and that, ultimately, the Lord's strength and power are what helped him through it.

Like it was for Paul, it was through the Lord's help that I was eventually strengthened emotionally and spiritually and finally recognized after many years that I have always been a person of worth and worthy of the blessings of the gospel. The Savior helped me to overcome my feelings of unworthiness and to extend sincere forgiveness to the offender.[9] I finally understood that the Savior's Atonement was a personal gift for me and that my Heavenly Father and His Son love me perfectly. Because of the Savior's Atonement, mortality works.

While I was eventually blessed to recognize how the Savior rescued me and stood by me through those experiences, I clearly understand that the unfortunate situation of my teenage years was *my* personal journey and experience, the resolution of which and eventual outcome cannot be projected onto those who have suffered and continue to suffer from the unrighteous behavior of others.

I recognize that life's experiences—good and bad—can teach us important lessons. I now know and bear testimony that mortality works! I hope that as a result of the sum of my life's experiences—good and bad—I have compassion for innocent victims of another's actions and empathy for the downtrodden.

I sincerely hope that as a result of my life's experiences—good and bad—I am kinder to others, treat others as the Savior would, and have greater understanding for the sinner and that I have complete integrity. As we come to rely on the Savior's grace and keep our covenants, we can serve as examples of the far-reaching effects of the Savior's Atonement.

I share a final example that mortality works.

My mother did not have an easy journey through mortality. She received no accolades or worldly honors and did not have educational opportunities beyond high school. She contracted polio as a child, resulting in a lifetime of pain and discomfort in her left leg. As an adult, she experienced many difficult and challenging physical and financial circumstances but was faithful to her covenants and loved the Lord.

When my mother was 55, my next older sister passed away, leaving an eight-month-old baby daughter, my niece, motherless. For various reasons, Mom ended up largely raising my niece for the next 17 years, often under very trying circumstances. Yet, notwithstanding these experiences, she happily and willingly served her family, neighbors, and ward members and served as an ordinance worker in the temple for many years. During the last several years of her life, Mom suffered from a form of dementia, was often confused, and was confined to a nursing facility. Regrettably, she was alone when she passed away unexpectedly.

Several months after her passing, I had a dream I have never forgotten. In my dream, I was sitting in my office at the Church Administration Building. Mom entered the office. I knew she had come from the spirit world. I will always remember the feelings I had. She did not say anything, but she radiated a spiritual beauty that I had never before experienced and which I have difficulty describing.

Her countenance and being were truly stunning! I remember saying to her, "Mother, you are so beautiful!," referencing her spiritual power and beauty. She acknowledged me—again without speaking. I felt her love for me, and I knew then that she is happy and healed from her worldly cares and challenges and eagerly awaits "a glorious resurrection."[10] I know that for Mom, mortality worked—and that it works for us too.

God's work and glory is to bring to pass the immortality and eternal life of man.[11] The experiences of mortality are part of the journey that allows us to grow and progress toward that immortality and eternal life. We were not sent here to fail but to succeed in God's plan for us.

As King Benjamin taught: "And moreover, I would desire that ye should consider on the blessed and happy state of those that keep the commandments of God. For behold, they are blessed in all things, both temporal and spiritual; and if they hold out faithful to the end they are received into heaven, that thereby they may dwell with God in a state of never-ending happiness."[12] In other words, mortality works!

I testify that as we receive the ordinances of the gospel, enter into covenants with God and then keep those covenants, repent, serve others, and endure to the end, we too can have the assurance and complete trust in the Lord that mortality works! I testify of Jesus Christ and that our glorious future with our Heavenly Father is made possible by the grace and Atonement of the Savior. In the name of Jesus Christ, amen.

Notes

1. Shared with permission. This experience accords with the Lord's teaching that death "shall be sweet unto" the righteous (Doctrine and Covenants 42:46). The Prophet Joseph Smith explained, "The spirits of the just are exalted to a greater and more glorious work . . . [in] the world of spirits" (*Teachings of Presidents of the Church: Joseph Smith* [2007], 179). He further taught, "They are not far from us, and know and understand our thoughts, feelings, and motions" (in Discourse, Oct. 9, 1843, as reported by *Times and Seasons*, 331, josephsmithpapers .org).

2. Moses 1:39.
3. Doctrine and Covenants 98:13–14.
4. Deuteronomy 8:2.
5. 2 Nephi 2:1–3.
6. "We Thank Thee, O God, for a Prophet," *Hymns*, no. 19.
7. Mosiah 23:22.
8. 2 Corinthians 12:7–9.
9. Elder Richard G. Scott said, "I testify that I know victims of serious abuse who have successfully made the difficult journey to full healing through the power of the Atonement" ("To Heal the Shattering Consequences of Abuse," *Ensign* or *Liahona*, May 2008, 40).
10. Doctrine and Covenants 138:14.
11. See Moses 1:39.
12. Mosiah 2:41.

SEEK HIM WITH ALL YOUR HEART

BISHOP L. TODD BUDGE
Second Counselor in the Presiding Bishopric

Several years ago, my wife and I served as mission leaders in Tokyo, Japan. During a visit to our mission by then-Elder Russell M. Nelson, one of the missionaries asked him how best to respond when a person tells them that they are too busy to listen to them. With little hesitation, Elder Nelson said, "I would ask if they were too busy to eat lunch that day and then teach them that they have both a body and a spirit, and just as their body will die if not nourished, so will their spirit if not nourished by the good word of God."

It is interesting to note that the Japanese word for "busy," *isogashii*, is made up of a character with two symbols (忙). The one on the left means "heart" or "spirit," and the one on the right means "death"—suggesting perhaps, as President Nelson taught, that being too busy to nourish our spirits can lead us to die spiritually.[1]

The Lord knew—in this fast-paced world full of distractions and in commotion—that making quality time for Him would be one of the major challenges of our day. Speaking through the prophet Isaiah, He provided these words of counsel and caution, which can be likened unto the tumultuous days in which we live:

"In *returning* and *rest* shall ye be saved; in *quietness* and in *confidence* shall be your strength: and ye would not.

"But ye said, No; for we will flee upon horses; therefore shall ye flee: and, We will ride upon the swift; therefore shall they that pursue you be swift."[2]

In other words, even though our salvation depends on *returning* to Him often and *resting* from the cares of the world, we do not. And even though our *confidence* will come from a strength developed in *quiet* times sitting with the Lord in meditation and reflection, we do not.[3] Why not? Because we say, "No, we are busy with other things"—fleeing upon our horses, so to speak. Therefore, we will get further and further away from God; we will insist on going faster and faster; and the faster we go, the swifter Satan will follow in pursuit.

Perhaps this is why President Nelson has repeatedly pled with us to make time for the Lord in our lives—"each and every day."[4] He reminds us that "quiet time is sacred time—time that will facilitate personal revelation and instill peace."[5] But to hear the still voice of the Lord, he counseled, "you too must be still."[6]

Being still, however, requires more than just making time for the Lord—it requires letting go of our doubtful and fearful thoughts and focusing our hearts and minds on Him. Elder David A. Bednar taught, "The Lord's admonition to 'be still' entails much more than simply not talking or not moving." To be still, he suggested, "may be a way of reminding us to focus upon the Savior unfailingly."[7]

Being still is an act of faith and requires effort.[8] *Lectures on Faith* states, "When a man works by faith he works by mental exertion."[9] President Nelson declared: "Our focus must be riveted on the Savior and His gospel. It is mentally rigorous to strive to look unto Him in *every* thought. But when we do, our doubts and fears flee."[10] Speaking of this need to focus our minds, President David O. McKay said: "I think we pay too little attention to the value of meditation, a principle of devotion. . . . Meditation is one of the . . . most sacred doors through which we pass into the presence of the Lord."[11]

There is a word in Japanese, *mui*, that, for me, captures this more faith-filled, contemplative sense of what it means to be still. It is comprised of two characters (無為). The one on the left means "nothing" or "nothingness," and the one on the right means "to do." Together they mean "non-doing." Taken literally, the word could be misinterpreted to mean "to do nothing" in the same way "to be still" can be misinterpreted as "not talking or moving." However, like the phrase "to be still," it has a higher meaning; for me it is a reminder to slow down and to live with greater spiritual awareness.

While serving in the Asia North Area Presidency with Elder Takashi Wada, I learned that his wife, Sister Naomi Wada, is an accomplished Japanese calligrapher. I asked Sister Wada if she would draw for me the Japanese characters for the word *mui*. I wanted to hang the calligraphy on my wall as a reminder to be still and to focus on the Savior. I was surprised when she did not readily agree to this seemingly simple request.

The next day, knowing that I had likely misunderstood her hesitance, Elder Wada explained that writing those characters would require a significant effort. She would need to ponder and meditate on the concept and the characters until she understood the meaning deeply in her soul and could give *expression* to these heartfelt *impressions* with each stroke of her brush. I was embarrassed that I had so casually asked her to do something so demanding. I asked him to convey my apologies to her for my ignorance and to let her know that I was withdrawing my request.

You can imagine my surprise and gratitude when upon my leaving Japan, Sister Wada, unsolicited, gifted to me [a] beautiful piece of calligraphy featuring the Japanese characters for the word *mui*. It now hangs prominently on the wall of my office, reminding me to be still and to seek the Lord every day with all my heart, might, mind, and strength.[12] She had captured, in this selfless act, the meaning of *mui*, or stillness, better than any words could. Rather than mindlessly and dutifully drawing the characters, she approached her calligraphy with full purpose of heart and real intent.

Likewise, God desires that we approach our time with Him with the same kind of heartfelt devotion.[13] When we do so, our worship becomes an expression of our love for Him.[14]

He yearns for us to commune with Him.[15] On one occasion, after I gave the invocation in a meeting with the First Presidency, President Nelson turned to me and said, "While you were praying, I thought how much God must appreciate when we take time from our busy schedules to acknowledge Him." It was a simple yet powerful reminder of how much it must mean to Heavenly Father when we pause to commune with Him.

As much as He desires our attention, He will not force us to come to Him. To the Nephites, the resurrected Lord said, "How oft *would I have* gathered you as a hen gathereth her chickens, and *ye* would not."[16] He followed that with this hopeful invitation that also applies to us today: "How oft *will* I gather you as a hen gathereth her chickens under her wings, if ye will repent and return[17] unto me with full purpose of heart."[18]

The gospel of Jesus Christ gives us opportunities to return to Him often. These opportunities include daily prayers, scripture study, the sacrament ordinance, the Sabbath day, and temple worship. What if we were to take these sacred opportunities off our to-do lists and put them on our "non-doing" lists—meaning to approach them with the same mindfulness and focus with which Sister Wada approaches her calligraphy?

You may be thinking, "I do not have time for that." I have often felt the same. But let me suggest that what may be needed is not necessarily more time but more awareness of and focus on God during the times we already set aside for Him.[19]

For example, when praying, what if we were to spend less time talking and more time just being with God;[20] and when we were to speak, to give more heartfelt and specific expressions of gratitude and love?[21]

President Nelson has counseled that we not just read the scriptures but savor them.[22] What difference would it make if we were to do less reading and more savoring?

What if we were to do more to prepare our minds to partake of the sacrament and joyfully pondered the blessings of the Atonement of Jesus Christ during this sacred ordinance?[23]

On the Sabbath, which in Hebrew means "rest," what if we were to rest from other cares and to take time to sit quietly with the Lord to pay our devotions unto Him?[24]

During our temple worship, what if we were to make a more disciplined effort to pay attention or lingered a little longer in the celestial room in quiet reflection?[25]

When our focus is less on doing and more on strengthening our covenant connection with Heavenly Father and Jesus Christ, I testify that each of these sacred moments will be enriched, and we will receive the guidance needed in our personal lives.[26] We, like Martha in the account in Luke, are often "careful and troubled about many things." However, as we commune with the Lord each day, He will help us to know that which is most needful.[27]

Even the Savior took time from His ministry to be still. The scriptures are replete with examples of the Lord retreating to a solitary place—a mountain, the wilderness, a desert place, or going "a little way off"—to pray to the Father.[28] If Jesus Christ sought quiet time to commune with God and to be strengthened by Him, it would be wise for us to do the same.

As we concentrate our hearts and minds on Heavenly Father and Jesus Christ and listen to the still, small voice of the Holy Ghost, we will have greater clarity about what is most needful, develop deeper compassion, and find rest and strength in Him. Paradoxically, helping God hasten His work of salvation and exaltation may require that we slow down.[29] Being always in motion may be adding to the commotion in our lives and robbing us of the peace we seek.

I testify that as we return often to the Lord with full purpose of heart, we will in *quietness* and *confidence* come to know Him and feel His infinite covenantal love for us.

The Lord promised:

"Draw near unto me and I will draw near unto you; seek me diligently and ye shall find me."[30]

"And ye shall seek me, and find me, when ye shall search for me with all your heart."[31]

I testify that this promise is true. In the name of Jesus Christ, amen.

Notes

1. See Ether 2:14–15.
2. Isaiah 30:15–16; emphasis added.
3. 2 Nephi 10:24 invites us to re-con-cile our will to God's will. "Re" means "again," "con" means "with," and "cile" is a chair or throne. To reconcile our will to God's can mean to literally sit again with God.
4. Russell M. Nelson, "Make Time for the Lord," *Liahona*, Nov. 2021, 120.
5. Russell M. Nelson, "What We Are Learning and Will Never Forget," *Liahona*, May 2021, 80.
6. Russell M. Nelson, "What We Are Learning and Will Never Forget," 80.
7. David A. Bednar, "Be Still, and Know That I Am God," *Liahona*, May 2024, 28.
8. See Hebrews 11:6.
9. *Lectures on Faith* (1985), 72.

10. Russell M. Nelson, "Drawing the Power of Jesus Christ into Our Lives," *Ensign* or *Liahona*, May 2017, 41.

11. David O. McKay, "Consciousness of God: Supreme Goal of Life," *Improvement Era*, June 1967, 80.

12. See Doctrine and Covenants 4:2.

13. See Mosiah 7:33; Ether 2:14.

14. "A healthy, functioning heart is central to the health and well-being of each of us. However, what I have learned as a servant and witness of Jesus Christ is that a healthy physical heart is only half of our challenge. I take seriously the injunction to love God with *all* our hearts, because loving Him is what keeps us vibrant" (Russell M. Nelson, *The Heart of the Matter: What 100 Years of Living Have Taught Me* [2023], 8; emphasis added).

15. See Psalm 14:2; Revelation 3:20.

16. 3 Nephi 10:5; emphasis added.

17. Elder Dale G. Renlund taught: "Changing our behavior and *returning* to the 'right road' are part of repentance, but only part. Real repentance also includes a *turning of our heart and will to God* and a renunciation of sin" ("Repentance: A Joyful Choice," *Ensign* or *Liahona*, Nov. 2016, 121; emphasis added).

18. 3 Nephi 10:6; emphasis added.

19. Elder Neal A. Maxwell taught, "Increased consecration is not so much a demand for more hours of Church work as it is for more awareness of whose work this really is!" ("Settle This in Your Hearts," *Ensign*, Nov. 1992, 67).

20. Commenting on how his prayers have evolved over time, Desmond Tutu stated: "I think [I am] trying to grow, in just being there. Like when you sit in front of a fire in winter—you are just there in front of the fire. You don't have to be smart or anything. The fire warms you" ("Desmond Tutu, Insisting We Are 'Made for Goodness'" [NPR interview by Renee Montagne, Mar. 11, 2010], npr.org).

21. See Russell M. Nelson, "Think Celestial!," *Liahona*, Nov. 2023, 117–19.

22. See Russell M. Nelson, "Living by Scriptural Guidance," *Ensign*, Nov. 2000, 16–18; or *Liahona*, Jan. 2001, 19–22; see also Russell M. Nelson, "The Answer Is Always Jesus Christ," *Liahona*, May 2023, 127–28.

23. See 3 Nephi 17:3. President David O. McKay declared:

    "I believe the short period of administering the sacrament is one of the best opportunities we have for such meditation, and there should be nothing during that sacred period to distract our attention from the purpose of that ordinance. . . .

    "I strongly urge that this sacred ordinance be surrounded with more reverence, with perfect order; that each one who comes to the house of God may meditate upon and silently and prayerfully express appreciation for God's goodness. . . . Let the sacrament hour be one experience of the day in which the worshiper tries at least to realize within himself that it is possible for him to commune with his God" ("Consciousness of God: Supreme Goal of Life," *Improvement Era*, June 1967, 80–81).

24. See Doctrine and Covenants 59:10.

25. "When you bring your temple recommend, a contrite heart, and a seeking mind to the Lord's house of learning, *He* will teach you" (Russell M. Nelson, "The Temple and Your Spiritual Foundation," *Liahona*, Nov. 2021, 95).

26. "He will lead and guide *you* in your personal life if you will *make time for Him* in your life—each and every day" (Russell M. Nelson, "Make Time for the Lord," 121).

27. See Luke 10:40–42.

28. 3 Nephi 19:19; see also Joseph Smith Translation, Matthew 4:1 (in Matthew 4:1, footnote *a*); Matthew 5:1; 14:13, 23; Mark 1:35; 6:46; Luke 5:16; 6:12.

29. See 3 Nephi 21:29.

30. Doctrine and Covenants 88:63.

31. Jeremiah 29:13; see also Lamentations 3:25.

DAYS NEVER TO BE FORGOTTEN

ELDER GARY E. STEVENSON
Of the Quorum of the Twelve Apostles

Introduction

My dear brothers and sisters, the history of The Church of Jesus Christ of Latter-day Saints in this dispensation is resplendent with divine experiences that demonstrate how the Lord has guided His Church. There is one decade in our history, however, that stands strikingly supreme above any other—the decade from 1820 to 1830. Beginning with the Prophet Joseph Smith's experience in the Sacred Grove in the spring of 1820, when he saw God the Father and His Son, Jesus Christ, and continuing until April 6, 1830, that decade is unlike any other.

Consider these remarkable events! The young prophet conversed with the angel Moroni, translated the gold plates, and published the Book of Mormon! He was the instrument through whom the Aaronic and Melchizedek Priesthoods were restored,[1] and then he organized the Church! Oliver Cowdery described that era well: "These were days never to be forgotten."[2] Miraculous events have continued to this very day.

May I be so bold as to suggest that this year we have commenced a decade that may prove to be as momentous as any that has followed that unparalleled founding decade almost two centuries ago.

Our Decade

Let me explain. Between now, 2024, and 2034, we will experience seminal events that will result in extraordinary opportunities to serve, to unite with members and friends, and to introduce The Church of Jesus Christ of Latter-day Saints to more people than ever before.

We just witnessed the power of a truly historic moment as we celebrated with tens of millions the 100th birthday of President Russell M. Nelson.

Reporting on President Nelson's birthday, *Newsweek* wrote a headline that read, "World's Oldest Religious Leader Turns 100." They then listed the world's 10 oldest faith leaders—with President Nelson first on a list that included Pope Francis and the Dalai Lama.[3]

This statement from a *New York Times* article represents the spirit of much of the international coverage: "In a [United States] presidential election cycle that has prompted soul-searching about aging and leadership, Mr. Nelson's milestone suggests that, at least in his church, a triple-digit birthday does not merit much hand-wringing. He remains a popular figure among church members, who view their president not just as an executive but as a 'prophet, seer, and revelator.'"[4]

How grateful we are that President Nelson's landmark birthday gave us an opportunity to introduce a global audience to a prophet of God, a celebration *never to be forgotten*.

Earlier this spring, a refurbished plaza on Temple Square—featuring a display of international flags representing countries where the Church is recognized—was unveiled. The plaza entrance is marked by a granite monument with these prophetic words: "And it shall come to pass in the last days, that the mountain of the Lord's house shall be established in the top of the mountains, and shall be exalted above the hills; and all nations shall flow unto it."[5]

Surely, the monumental events that will occur during the next 10 years constitute one manifestation this prophecy of Isaiah is being fulfilled.

Contemplate the unprecedented number of temple open houses and dedications that are planned to take place over the next decade, even the potential of 164 temples and counting. Imagine tens of millions of you and your friends walking through a house of the Lord. The symbolic center of these events will be the rededication of the Salt Lake Temple and the activities associated with it. These certainly will be days never to be forgotten.

The year 2030 will bring opportunities worldwide to commemorate the bicentennial of the organization of the Church. Although it is too early to say how the Church will recognize this milestone, it will certainly allow us to invite family, friends, colleagues, and distinguished guests to "come and see"[6] and to better understand the powerful impact the Church has in the lives of Church members.

In 2034, thousands of dignitaries, visitors, and athletes from around the world will flood the streets of Salt Lake City, the stage for the Winter Olympic Games. There is perhaps no greater demonstration of worldwide unity than that embodied in the Olympic Games. The eyes of the world will be upon the Church and its members, affording a multitude of opportunities to volunteer, serve, and share glad tidings through kind deeds—an event never to be forgotten.

These upcoming moments will provide members of the Church everywhere with increased opportunities to share the glad tidings of the gospel of Jesus Christ through word and deed, a decade never to be forgotten.

Glad Tidings

In a meeting just weeks before his birthday, President Nelson shared the reason he cherishes the phrase "glad tidings." On the face of it, he noted, the phrase rings of joy and happiness. But "glad tidings" conveys much more than that. He explained that this phrase comes from the original Greek word *euangelion*, which literally means the "good news" or the "gospel."[7] Happiness and joy in this life and the next are always linked with the gospel of Jesus Christ. Thus the phrase "glad tidings" captures this double meaning in a wonderful way.

"Men [and women] are, that they might have joy."[8] Heavenly Father has provided the plan of happiness that enables joy through His blessings. These include living in His presence eternally as families. The Atonement of Jesus Christ is central to God's plan to redeem us. To receive eternal life, we must come unto Christ. As we do so "and help others do the same, we participate in God's work of salvation and exaltation."[9]

This message of the glad tidings of the gospel of Jesus Christ is the most important message on earth. And that is where the youth and young adults of the Church come in.

For the Strength of Youth

Now, while this upcoming decade may be filled with days *never to be forgotten* for every member of the Church, this especially can be true for you of the rising generation. You are here on earth now because you were selected to be here now. You have the strength and capacity to be disciples of Christ in an unprecedented way.

President George Q. Cannon taught, "God has reserved spirits for this dispensation who have the courage and determination to face the world and all the powers of the evil one [and to] . . . build up the Zion of our God fearless of all consequences."[10]

To that end, I wish to speak to you of the rising generation, to invite you to imagine how exciting this next decade, one never to be forgotten, can be *for you*. I also offer a few simple words of counsel and encouragement that may empower you during this coming decade.

Like many of you, I have a smartphone that, on occasion and without any prompt, pulls together a reel of photos showing what I was doing on a certain day. It is always surprising to see how much things have changed for me and my family in just a few years.

Picture the photos *your* phone will serve up 10 years from now! You may see yourself graduating from high school or college, receiving your endowment, going on a mission, getting married, and having your first child. For you personally, this will be a decade *never to be forgotten*. But it will be *doubly* so if you actively strive to become a light unto the world of how the glad tidings of the gospel of Jesus Christ can enrich and enhance not only your lives but also those of your family, friends, and social media followers.

You may be wondering how to do this.

Prophets of God have taught us this is done through four simple activities, referred to as divinely appointed responsibilities:[11] first, living the gospel of Jesus Christ; second, caring for those in need; third, inviting all to receive the gospel; and fourth, uniting families for eternity. Remarkably, each can be done in the most normal and natural ways.

Divinely Appointed Responsibilities

I promise you this will be a decade never to be forgotten *for you* if you embrace these four divinely appointed responsibilities. Let's consider what this might entail.

First, live the gospel of Jesus Christ. Study the words of the prophets, and learn to love your Father in Heaven. Incline your hearts to Him, and strive to walk in His way. Be lifted by the "covenant confidence" that Elder Ulisses Soares has described.[12] This confidence comes from making covenants to follow Jesus Christ, knowing that the Savior will in turn strengthen and support you.

Let your friends see the joy you feel in living the gospel, and you will be the best gospel message they ever receive.

Second, reach out in compassion to care for those in need. Your generation is unusually mindful of the less fortunate. Whenever disaster strikes and Church members rush to help clear away debris and comfort the afflicted, it seems the majority wearing "Helping Hands" T-shirts are teenagers and twentysomethings. It is in your nature "to bear one another's burdens" and "comfort those that stand in need of comfort."[13] By doing this we "fulfil the law of Christ."[14]

Evan, a young Primary-age boy, decided to spend his summer vacation from school gathering supplies for peanut butter and jelly sandwiches to donate to his local food bank. He found the project on the JustServe website. Young Evan enlisted his entire school class to help collect over 700 jars of jelly![15] Let the people you serve know that your concern for them is rooted in your love of God and your desire to treat your neighbor as yourself.[16]

Third, invite all to receive the gospel. This year we opened 36 new missions worldwide to accommodate all who desire to serve full-time missions. In an era when many youth are opting out of formal religious activity altogether, this is remarkable and speaks to the magnificent nature of your testimonies. Whether serving full-time or not, please realize your immense capacity to influence your peers as you love, share, and invite them to explore the gospel of Jesus Christ.

Fourth, unite families for eternity. As I visit temples around the world, I marvel at the standing-room-only crowds of youth waiting at the baptistry and the increased numbers of young adults serving as ordinance workers. Recently a group of over 600 youth from Scotland and Ireland traveled to the Preston England Temple, performing over 4,000 ordinances, many of which were for their personal deceased ancestors![17] I urge you to become engaged in family history, spend time in the temple, and carefully prepare yourself to be the kind of man or woman ready to marry an equally worthy companion in the temple. Develop a pattern in your life *now* to make the temple a regular part of your lives.

Conclusion

My beloved brothers and sisters, my dear young friends, there will likely be difficulties for each of us in the days ahead. However, as we enter this coming decade of unprecedented moments, may we share glad tidings through the simple activities of living, caring, inviting, and uniting. As we do so, the Lord will bless us with experiences never to be forgotten.

I testify that those who approach the Lord with a sincere heart and real intent, those who have the name of the Savior upon their lips and the Holy Spirit in their souls, those who embark upon this grand and glorious pilgrimage will discover and experience bounteous celestial blessings and receive a witness that God hears you, knows you, and loves you. You will experience days never to be forgotten. In the name of Jesus Christ, amen.

Notes

1. See Doctrine and Covenants 27:8, 12–13.
2. Joseph Smith—History 1:71, note.
3. See Theo Burman, "World's Oldest Religious Leader Turns 100," *Newsweek*, Sept. 9, 2024, newsweek.com.
4. Ruth Graham, "The Leader of the Mormon Church Turns 100," *New York Times*, Sept. 9, 2024, nytimes.com. An Associated Press article quoted a leader at Duke University's Divinity School as saying, "Age, wisdom and spiritual authority go together" (Angie Hong, in Hannah Schoenbaum and Deepa Bharath, "The Mormon Church's Oldest-Ever President Has Turned 100," Sept. 9, 2024, apnews.com).
5. Isaiah 2:2.
6. John 1:46.
7. See James Strong, *The New Strong's Exhaustive Concordance of the Bible* (1984), Greek dictionary section, entry 2098.
8. 2 Nephi 2:25.

9. *General Handbook: Serving in The Church of Jesus Christ of Latter-day Saints*, 1.2, Gospel Library.

10. *Gospel Truth: Discourses and Writings of President George Q. Cannon*, sel. Jerreld L. Newquist (1957), 1:21.

11. See *General Handbook*, 1.2, Gospel Library.

12. See Ulisses Soares, "Covenant Confidence through Jesus Christ," *Liahona*, May 2024, 17–21.

13. Mosiah 18:8, 9.

14. Galatians 6:2.

15. See Jessica Lawrence, "Finding Joy in Donating Jelly," *Church News*, June 18, 2023, thechurch-news.com.

16. See Matthew 22:37–40.

17. See Melina Myers, "Scottish and Irish Youth Perform over 4,000 Ordinances in the Preston England Temple," *Church News*, June 13, 2024, thechurchnews.com.

O YOUTH OF THE NOBLE BIRTHRIGHT

BROTHER BRADLEY R. WILCOX
First Counselor in the Young Men General Presidency

Elder Stevenson, this is a conference never to be forgotten.

Our family has always enjoyed a little book called *Children's Letters to God*. Here are a few:

"Dear God, instead of letting people die and having to make new ones, why don't you just keep the ones you've got right now?"

"How come you only have ten rules, but our school has millions?"

"Why did you put the tonsils in if you're just going to take them out again?"[1]

Today there isn't time to answer all *these* questions, but there is another question I often hear from young people that I would like to address. From Ulaanbaatar, Mongolia, to Thomas, Idaho, the question is the same: "Why? Why must Latter-day Saints live so differently from others?"

I know it's hard to be different—especially when you are young and want so badly for other people to like you. Everyone wants to fit in, and that desire is magnified to unhealthy proportions in today's digital world filled with social media and cyberbullying.

So, with all that pressure, why *do* Latter-day Saints live so differently? There are many good answers: Because you are a child of God. Because you have been saved for the last days. Because you are a disciple of Jesus Christ.

But those answers don't always set you apart. Everyone is a child of God. Everyone on earth right now was sent here in the latter days. And yet not everyone lives the Word of Wisdom or law of chastity the way you strive to. There are many valiant disciples of Christ who are not members of this Church. But they do not serve missions and perform ordinances in houses of the Lord on behalf of ancestors like you do. There must be more to it—and there is.

Today I would like to focus on an additional reason that has been meaningful in my life. In 1988 a young Apostle named

Russell M. Nelson gave an address at Brigham Young University called "Thanks for the Covenant."[2] In it, then-Elder Nelson explained that when we use our moral agency to make and keep covenants with God, we become heirs of the everlasting covenant God has made with our forebearers in every dispensation. Said another way, we become "children of the covenant."[3] That sets us apart. That gives us access to the same blessings our forefathers and foremothers received, including a birthright.[4]

Birthright! You may have heard that word. We even sing hymns about it: "O youth of the noble birthright, carry on, carry on, carry on!"[5] It's a compelling word. But what does it mean?

In Old Testament times if a father passed away, his birthright son was responsible for the care of his mother and sisters. His brothers received their inheritance and left to make their way in the world, but the birthright son did not go anywhere. He would marry and have his own family, but he would stay until the end of his days to govern the affairs of his father's estate.[6] Because of this added responsibility, he was given an added measure of the inheritance. Was leading and caring for others too much to ask? Not when you consider the additional inheritance he was given.[7]

Today we are not talking about your birth order in earthly families or Old Testament gender roles. We are talking about the inheritance you receive as a joint heir with Christ[8] because of the covenant relationship you have chosen to enter with Him and your Father in Heaven. Is it too much for God to expect you to live differently than His other children so you can better lead and serve them? Not when you consider the blessings—both temporal and spiritual—that you have been given.[9]

Does your birthright mean you are better than others? No, but it does mean you are expected to help others be better. Does your birthright mean you are chosen? Yes,[10] but not chosen to rule over others; you are chosen to serve them.[11] Is your birthright evidence of God's love? Yes, but more important, it is evidence of His trust.[12]

It is one thing to be loved and another thing entirely to be trusted. In the *For the Strength of Youth* guide, we read: "Your Father in Heaven trusts you. He has given you great blessings, including the fulness of the gospel and sacred ordinances and covenants that bind you to Him and bring His power into your life. With those blessings comes added responsibility. He knows you can make a difference in the world, and that requires, in many cases, being different from the world."[13]

Our mortal experience could be compared to a cruise ship on which God has sent all His children as they journey from one shore to another. The voyage is filled with opportunities to learn, grow, be happy, and progress, but it is also full of dangers. God loves all His children and is concerned about their welfare. He does not want to lose any of them, so He invites those who are willing[14] to become members of His crew—that's you. Because of your choice to make and keep covenants, He offers you His trust. He trusts you to be different, peculiar, and set apart[15] because of the important work He trusts you to do.[16]

Think of it! God trusts you—of all the people on the earth, the children of the covenant, His crew members—to help with His work of bringing all His children safely home to Him. No wonder President Brigham Young once said, "All the angels in heaven are looking at this little handful of people."[17]

When you look around on this cruise ship called earth, you might see other people sitting in lounge chairs drinking, gambling in casinos, wearing clothing that is too revealing, scrolling endlessly on cell phones, and wasting too much time playing electronic games. But instead of wondering, "Why can't *I* do that?," you can remember that you are not an ordinary passenger. You are a member of the crew. You have responsibilities that passengers do not have. As Sister Ardeth Kapp once said, "You can't be a life[guard] if you look like all the other swimmers on the beach."[18]

And before you become discouraged by all the extra obligations, please remember that crew members receive something the other passengers do not: compensation.[19] Elder Neil L. Andersen has said, "There is a compensatory spiritual power for the righteous," including "greater assurance, greater confirmation, and greater confidence."[20] Like Abraham of old, you receive greater happiness and peace, greater righteousness, and greater knowledge.[21] Your compensation is not merely a mansion in heaven and streets paved with gold. It would be easy for Heavenly Father to simply give you all that He has. His desire is to help you become all that He is.[22] Thus, your commitments demand more of you because that is how God is making more of you.

It's "a lot to ask of anyone, but you're not just anyone"![23] You are youth of the noble birthright. Your covenant relationship with God and Jesus Christ is a relationship of love and trust[24] in which you have access to a greater measure of Their grace—Their divine assistance, endowment of strength, and enabling power.[25] That power is not just wishful thinking, a lucky charm, or self-fulfilling prophecy. It is *real*.

As you fulfill your birthright responsibilities, you are never alone. The Lord of the vineyard labors with you.[26] You are working hand in hand with Jesus Christ. With each new covenant—and as your relationship with Him deepens—you hold each other tighter and tighter until you are firmly clasped together.[27] In that sacred symbol of His grace, you will find both the desire and the strength to live exactly how the Savior lived—differently from the world. You've got this because Jesus Christ has got you![28]

In 2 Nephi 2:6 we read, "Wherefore, redemption cometh in and through the Holy Messiah; for he is full of grace and truth." Because He is full of truth, He sees you as you really are—flaws, weaknesses, regrets, and all. Because He is full of grace, He sees you as you really can be. He meets you where you are and helps you repent and improve, overcome and become.

"O youth of the noble birthright, carry on, carry on, carry on!"[29] I testify that you are loved—and you are trusted—today, in 20 years, and forever. Don't sell your birthright for a mess of pottage.[30] Don't trade everything for nothing.[31] Don't let the world change you when you were born to change the world. In the name of Jesus Christ, amen.

Notes

1. In Stuart Hample and Eric Marshall, *Children's Letters to God* (1991).
2. See Russell M. Nelson, "Thanks for the Covenant" (Brigham Young University devotional, Nov. 22, 1988), speeches.byu.edu.
3. 3 Nephi 20:26; see also Russell M. Nelson, "Choices for Eternity" (worldwide devotional for young adults, May 15, 2022), Gospel Library; Russell M. Nelson, "Children of the Covenant," *Ensign*, May 1995, 32–35.
4. See 3 Nephi 20:25; see also Guide to the Scriptures, "Abrahamic Covenant," Gospel Library; Abraham 2:6 (promised land: celestial glory, eternal families); Genesis 13:16; Doctrine and Covenants 132:30–31 (posterity: eternal increase); and Abraham 1:18; 2:11 (priesthood: authority, keys, ordinances, covenants, and divine power); Russell M. Nelson, "Rejoice in the Gift of Priesthood Keys," *Liahona*, May 2024, 119–23.
5. "Carry On," *Hymns*, no. 255.
6. See Russell M. Nelson, "Youth of the Noble Birthright: What Will You Choose?" (Church Educational System devotional for young adults, Sept. 6, 2013), Gospel Library; see also Russell M. Nelson, "Thanks for the Covenant," speeches.byu.edu; Guide to the Scriptures, "Firstborn," Gospel Library.
7. See Luke 12:42; 17:7–10.
8. See Romans 8:17; see also Doctrine and Covenants 76:54–55; 88:107.
9. The Lord said, "It is a light thing" (1 Nephi 21:6).
10. See 1 Peter 2:9.
11. The Lord said, "Thou art my servant, O Israel" (1 Nephi 21:3).
12. See Exodus 2:25.
13. *For the Strength of Youth: A Guide for Making Choices* (2022), 4; see also Doctrine and Covenants 84:18–25; 107:18–21; Russell M. Nelson, "Youth of the Noble Birthright: What Will You Choose?"
14. See Doctrine and Covenants 20:77.
15. See 1 Peter 2:9.
16. See Moses 1:6; see also "Aaronic Priesthood Quorum Theme," Gospel Library.
17. *Teachings of Presidents of the Church: Brigham Young* (1997), 309.
18. Ardeth Greene Kapp, *I Walk by Faith* (1987), 97.
19. See Mosiah 2:22, 41; Doctrine and Covenants 59:23.
20. Neil L. Andersen, "A Compensatory Spiritual Power for the Righteous" (Brigham Young University devotional, Aug. 18, 2015), 3, speeches.byu.edu.
21. See Abraham 1:2.
22. See Dallin H. Oaks, *With Full Purpose of Heart* (2002), 38.
23. Kenneth Cope, "The Best for Last," *Voices* (album, 1991).
24. See Alma 53:20; 57:27.
25. See Dieter F. Uchtdorf, "The Gift of Grace," *Ensign* or *Liahona*, May 2015, 107; see also Guide to the Scriptures, "Grace," Gospel Library. I used to be confused by the many descriptions of God's power found throughout the scriptures. They speak of grace as enabling power (see Philippians 4:13) but also the Light of Christ as power (see Doctrine and Covenant 88:13). We read of the power of faith (see Alma 18:35), the power of the Holy Ghost (see Moroni 10:7), and power from on high promised in temples (see Doctrine and Covenants 38:32; 105:11). Scriptures also teach of the power of the priesthood (see Doctrine and Covenants 113:8). I couldn't figure out where one ended and the others began. Finally, I realized that "there is no other power, save the power of God" (Doctrine and Covenants 8:7; see also Romans 13:1). Different labels for God's power do not describe different powers but varying amounts, uses, and aspects of the same power.
26. See Jacob 5:72.
27. See Jacob 6:5.
28. See 3 Nephi 22:17.
29. *Hymns*, no. 255.
30. See Genesis 25:29–34.
31. See 3 Nephi 20:38; see also Isaiah 55:2.

SIMPLE IS THE DOCTRINE OF JESUS CHRIST

PRESIDENT HENRY B. EYRING
Second Counselor in the First Presidency

All of us have family members we love who are being tempted and tried by the seemingly constant forces of Satan, the destroyer, who would make all God's children miserable. For many of us, there have been sleepless nights. We have tried to surround the people who are at risk with every force for good. We have pled in prayer for them. We have loved them. We have set the best example we could.

Alma, a wise prophet from ancient times, faced similar trials. The people he led and loved were frequently under attack by a ferocious enemy, yet they were still trying to rear righteous children in a world of wickedness. Alma felt his only hope of victory was a force which at times we underestimate and often use too little. He pled for God's help.

Alma knew that for God to help, repentance was required by those he led, as well as his adversaries. Thus, he opted for a different approach to battle.

The Book of Mormon describes it this way: "And now, as the preaching of the word had a great tendency to lead the people to do that which was just—yea, it had . . . more powerful effect upon the minds of the people than the sword, or anything else, which had happened unto them—therefore Alma thought it was expedient that they should try the virtue of the word of God."[1]

The word of God is the doctrine taught by Jesus Christ and by His prophets. Alma knew that the words of doctrine had great power.

In the 18th section of the Doctrine and Covenants, the Lord revealed the foundation of His doctrine:

"For, behold, I command all men everywhere to repent. . . .

"For, behold, the Lord your Redeemer suffered death in the flesh; wherefore he suffered the pain of all men, that all men might repent and come unto him.

"And he hath risen again from the dead, that he might bring all men unto him, on conditions of repentance."[2]

"And you shall fall down and worship the Father in my name.

" . . . You must repent and be baptized, in the name of Jesus Christ."[3]

"Ask the Father in my name in faith, believing that you shall receive, and you shall have the Holy Ghost."[4]

"And now, after . . . you have received this, you must keep my commandments in all things."[5]

"Take upon you the name of Christ, and speak the truth in soberness.

"And as many as repent and are baptized in my name, which is Jesus Christ, and endure to the end, the same shall be saved."[6]

In those few passages, the Savior gives us the perfect example of how we should teach His doctrine. This doctrine is that faith in the Lord Jesus Christ, repentance, baptism, receiving the gift of the Holy Ghost, and enduring to the end blesses all of God's children.

As we teach these principles to those we love, the Holy Ghost will help us to know the truth. Because we need the promptings of the Holy Ghost, we must avoid speculation or personal interpretation that goes beyond teaching true doctrine.

That can be hard to do when you love the person you are trying to influence. He or she may have ignored the doctrine that has been taught. It is tempting to try something new or sensational. But the Holy Ghost will reveal the spirit of truth only as we are cautious and careful not to go beyond teaching true doctrine. One of the surest ways to avoid even getting near false doctrine is to choose to be simple in our teaching. Safety is gained by that simplicity, and little is lost.

Teaching simply allows us to share the saving doctrine early on, while children remain untouched by the deceiver's temptations that will later confront them, long before the truths they need to learn are drowned out by the noise of social media, peers, and their own personal struggles. We should seize every opportunity to share the teachings of Jesus Christ with children. These teaching moments are precious and far fewer compared to the relentless efforts of opposing forces. For every hour spent instilling doctrine into a child's life, there are countless hours of opposition filled with messages and images that challenge or ignore those saving truths.

Some of you may wonder whether it might be better to draw your children closer to you through having fun, or you may ask whether the child may start to feel overwhelmed by your teachings. Instead, we should consider, "With so little time and so few opportunities, what words of doctrine can I share that will strengthen them against the inevitable challenges to their faith?" The words you share today could be the ones they carry with them, and today will soon pass.

I have always admired my great-grandmother Mary Bommeli's devotion to sharing the doctrine of Jesus Christ. Her family was taught by missionaries in Switzerland when she was 24.

After being baptized, Mary desired to join the Saints in America, so she made her way from Switzerland to Berlin and found work with a woman who employed her to weave cloth for the family's clothing. Mary lived in a servant's room and set up her loom in the home's living area.

At that time, teaching the doctrine of The Church of Jesus Christ of Latter-day Saints was illegal in Berlin. But Mary found she could not keep from sharing the things she had learned. The woman of the house and her friends would gather around the loom to hear Mary teach. She spoke of the appearance of Heavenly Father and Jesus Christ to Joseph Smith, the visitation of angels, and the Book of Mormon. Remembering the accounts of Alma, she taught about the doctrine of the Resurrection. She testified that families can be reunited in the celestial kingdom.

Mary's enthusiasm to share the doctrine of the restored gospel soon caused trouble. It was not long before the police took Mary off to jail. On the way, she asked the policeman for the name of the judge she was to appear before the next morning. She also asked about his family and if he was a good father and husband. The policeman described the judge as a man of the world.

In the jail, Mary requested a pencil and some paper. She spent the night writing a letter to the judge, bearing witness to the Resurrection of Jesus Christ as described in the Book of Mormon, discussing the spirit world, and explaining repentance. She suggested that the judge would need time to reflect on his life before facing final judgment. She wrote that she knew he had much to repent of, much which would deeply sadden his family and bring him great sorrow. In the morning, when she had finished her letter, she gave it to the policeman and asked him to deliver it to the judge, and he agreed to do so.

Later, the policeman was summoned by the judge to his office. The letter Mary had written was irrefutable evidence that she was teaching the doctrine of the restored gospel and, by so doing, breaking the law. However, it wasn't long before the policeman returned to Mary's cell. He told her that all charges were dismissed and that she was free to go. Her teaching the doctrine of the restored gospel of Jesus Christ had caused her to be cast into jail. And her declaring the doctrine of repentance to the judge got her cast out of jail.[7]

Mary Bommeli's teaching did not end with her release. The record of her words passed true doctrine down through generations yet unborn. Her belief that even a new convert could teach the doctrine of Jesus Christ has ensured that her descendants will be strengthened in their own battles.

As we do our best to teach those we love about the doctrine of Jesus Christ, some may still not respond. Doubts may creep into your mind. You might question whether you know the Savior's doctrine well enough to teach it effectively. And if you've already made attempts to teach it, you may wonder why the positive effects aren't more visible. Don't give in to those doubts. Turn to God for help.

"Yea, and cry unto God for all thy support; . . . let the affections of thy heart be placed upon the Lord forever."[8]

"And now I would that ye should be humble, and be submissive and gentle; easy to be entreated; full of patience and long-suffering; being temperate in all things; being diligent in keeping the commandments of God at all times; asking for whatsoever things ye stand in need, both spiritual and temporal; always returning thanks unto God for whatsoever things ye do receive."[9]

If you pray, if you talk to God, and if you plead for His help for your loved one, and if you thank Him not only for help but for the patience and gentleness that come from not receiving all you desire right away or perhaps ever, then I promise you that you will draw closer to Him. You will become diligent and long-suffering. And then you can know that you have done all that you can to help those you love and those you pray for navigate through Satan's attempt to derail them.

"But they that wait upon the Lord shall renew their strength; they shall mount up with wings as eagles; they shall run, and not be weary; and they shall walk, and not faint."[10]

You can find hope in the scriptural record of families. We read of those who turned away from what they were taught or who were wrestling with God for forgiveness, such as Alma the Younger, the sons of Mosiah, and Enos. In their moments of crisis, they remembered the words of their parents, words of the doctrine of Jesus Christ. Remembering saved them. Your teaching of that sacred doctrine will be remembered.

I bear witness of the sacred work of teaching Heavenly Father's children the simple doctrine of Jesus Christ, which allows us to be spiritually cleansed and ultimately be welcomed into God's presence, to live with Him and His Son in glory forever in families. In the name of Jesus Christ, amen.

Notes

1. Alma 31:5.
2. Doctrine and Covenants 18:9, 11–12.
3. Doctrine and Covenants 18:40–41.
4. Doctrine and Covenants 18:18.
5. Doctrine and Covenants 18:43.
6. Doctrine and Covenants 18:21–22.
7. See Theresa Snow Hill, *Life and Times of Henry Eyring and Mary Bommeli* (1997), 15–22.
8. Alma 37:36.
9. Alma 7:23.
10. Isaiah 40:31.

Sunday Afternoon Session

OCTOBER 6, 2024

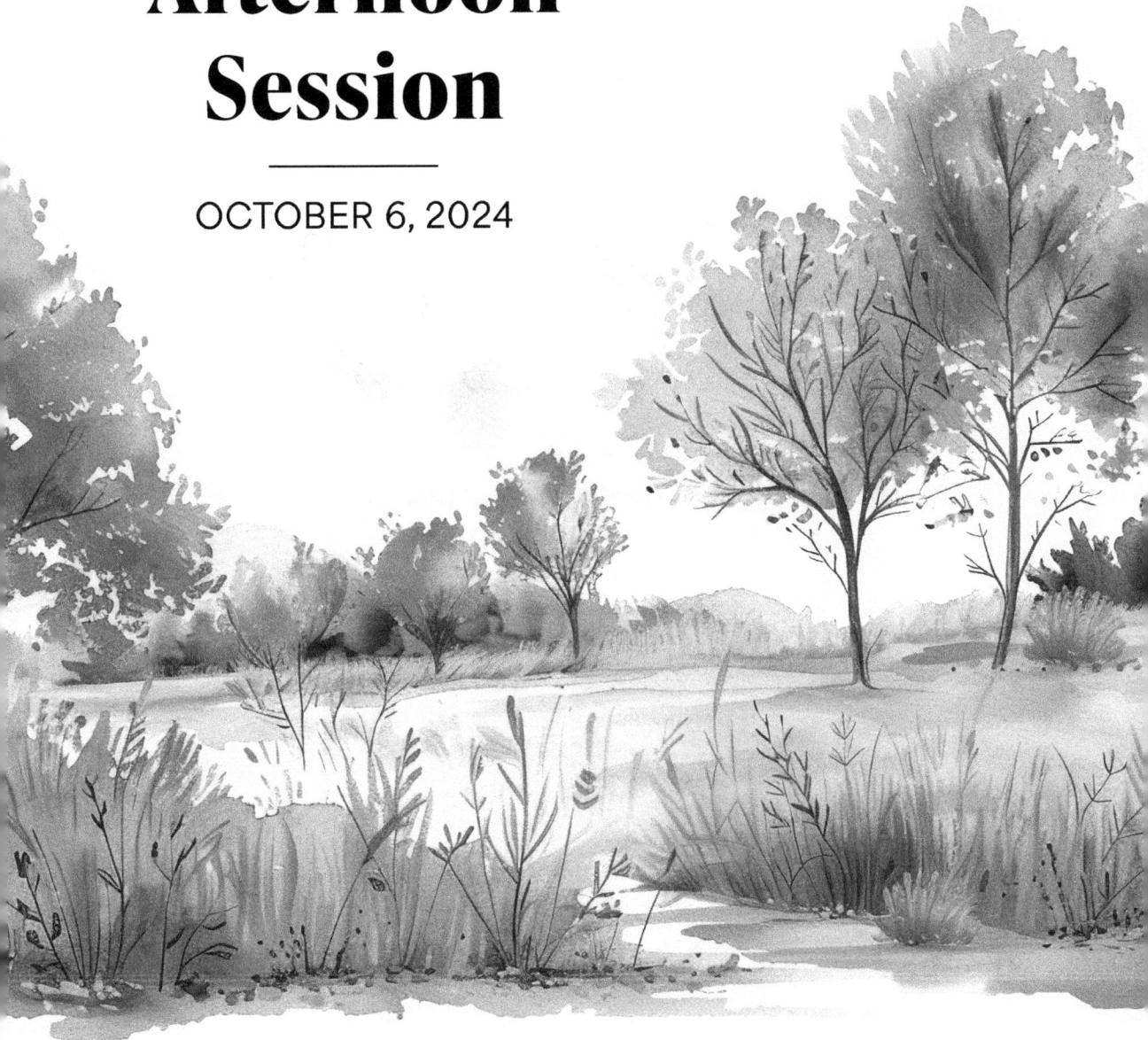

NOURISH THE ROOTS, AND THE BRANCHES WILL GROW

ELDER DIETER F. UCHTDORF
Of the Quorum of the Twelve Apostles

An Old Chapel in Zwickau

The year 2024 is something of a milestone year for me. It marks 75 years since I was baptized and confirmed a member of The Church of Jesus Christ of Latter-day Saints in Zwickau, Germany.[1]

My membership in the Church of Jesus Christ is precious to me. To be counted among God's covenant people, with you, my brothers and sisters, is one of the greatest honors of my life.

When I think about my personal journey of discipleship, my mind often goes back to an old villa in Zwickau, where I have cherished memories of attending sacrament meetings of the Church of Jesus Christ as a child. It is there where the seedling of my testimony received its earliest nourishing.[2]

This chapel had an old air-driven organ. Every Sunday a young man was assigned to push up and down the sturdy lever operating the bellows to make the organ work. I sometimes had the great privilege of assisting in this important task.

While the congregation sang our beloved hymns, I pumped with all my strength so the organ would not run out of wind. From the bellows operator seat, I had a great view of some stunning stained-glass windows, one depicting the Savior Jesus Christ and another portraying Joseph Smith in the Sacred Grove.

I can still remember the sacred feelings I had as I looked at those sunlit windows while listening to the testimonies of the Saints and singing the hymns of Zion.

In that holy place, the Spirit of God bore witness to my mind and heart that it was true: Jesus Christ is the Savior of the world. This is His Church. The Prophet Joseph Smith saw God the Father and Jesus Christ and heard Their voices.

Earlier this year, while on assignment in Europe, I had the

opportunity to return to Zwickau. Sadly, that beloved old chapel isn't there anymore. It was torn down many years ago to make room for a large apartment building.

What Is Eternal, and What Is Not?

I admit that it's sad to know that this beloved building from my childhood is now just a memory. It was a sacred building to me. But it was just a building.

By contrast, the spiritual witness I gained from the Holy Ghost those many years ago has not passed away. In fact, it has grown stronger. The things I learned in my youth about the fundamental principles of the gospel of Jesus Christ have been my firm foundation throughout my life. The covenant connection I forged with my Heavenly Father and His Beloved Son has stayed with me—long after the Zwickau chapel was dismantled and the stained-glass windows were lost.

"Heaven and earth shall pass away," Jesus said, "but my words shall not pass away."[3]

"The mountains shall depart, and the hills be removed; but my kindness shall not depart from thee, neither shall the covenant of my peace be removed, saith the Lord."[4]

One of the most important things we can learn in this life is the difference between what is eternal and what is not.[5] Once we understand that, everything changes—our relationships, the choices we make, the way we treat people.

Knowing what is eternal and what is not is key to growing a testimony of Jesus Christ and His Church.

Don't Mistake the Branches for the Roots

The restored gospel of Jesus Christ, as the Prophet Joseph Smith taught, "embrace[s] all, and every item of truth."[6] But that doesn't mean that all truth is of equal value. Some truths are core, essential, at the root of our faith. Others are appendages or branches—valuable, but only when they are connected to the fundamentals.

The Prophet Joseph also said, "The fundamental principles of our religion are the testimony of the Apostles and Prophets, concerning Jesus Christ, that He died, was buried, and rose again the third day, and ascended into heaven; and all other things which pertain to our religion are only appendages to it."[7]

In other words, Jesus Christ and His atoning sacrifice are the root of our testimony. All other things are branches.

This is not to say that the branches are unimportant. A tree needs branches. But as the Savior told His disciples, "The branch cannot bear fruit of itself, except it abide in the vine."[8] Without a connection to the Savior, to the nourishment found in the roots, a branch withers and dies.

When it comes to nourishing our testimonies of Jesus Christ, I wonder if we sometimes mistake the branches for the roots. This was the mistake Jesus observed in the Pharisees of His day. They paid so much attention to the relatively minor details of the law that they ended up neglecting what the Savior called "the weightier matters"—fundamental principles like "justice and mercy and faith."[9]

If you want to nourish a tree, you don't splash water on the branches. You water the roots. Similarly, if you want the branches of your testimony to grow and bear fruit, nourish the roots. If you are uncertain about a particular doctrine or practice or element of Church history, seek clarity with faith in Jesus Christ. Seek to understand His sacrifice for you, His love for you, His will for you. Follow Him in humility. The branches of your testimony will draw strength from your deepening faith in Heavenly Father and His Beloved Son.

For example, if you want a stronger testimony of the Book of Mormon, focus on its witness of Jesus Christ. Notice how the Book of Mormon testifies of Him, what it teaches about Him, and how it invites and inspires you to come unto Him.[10]

If you're seeking a more meaningful experience in Church meetings or in the temple, try looking for the Savior in the sacred ordinances we receive there.[11] Find the Lord in His holy house.

If you ever feel burned out or overwhelmed by your Church calling, try refocusing your service on Jesus Christ. Make it an expression of your love for Him.[12]

Nourish the roots, and the branches will grow. And in time, they will bear fruit.

Rooted and Built Up in Him

Strong faith in Jesus Christ doesn't happen overnight. No, in this mortal world, it's the thorns and thistles of doubt that grow spontaneously.[13] The healthy, fruitful tree of faith requires intentional effort.[14] And a vital part of that effort is making sure we are firmly rooted in Christ.

For example: At first, we may be drawn to the Savior's gospel and Church because we are impressed by the friendly members or by the kind bishop or the clean looks of the chapel. These circumstances are certainly important to grow the Church.

Nevertheless, if the roots of our testimony never grow deeper than that, what will happen when we move to a ward that meets in a less impressive building, with members who aren't so friendly, and the bishop says something that offends us?

Another example: Doesn't it seem reasonable to hope that if we keep the commandments and are sealed in the temple, we will be blessed with a large, happy family with bright, obedient children, all of whom stay active in the Church, serve missions, sing in the ward choir, and volunteer to help clean the meetinghouse every Saturday morning?

I certainly hope that all of us will see this in our lives. But what if it doesn't happen? Will we stay bound to the Savior regardless of circumstances—trusting Him and His timing?

We must ask ourselves: Is my testimony based on what I hope to happen in my life? Is it dependent on the actions or attitudes of others? Or is it firmly founded on Jesus Christ, "rooted and built up in him,"[15] regardless of life's changing circumstances?

Traditions, Habits, and Faith

The Book of Mormon tells of a people who "were strict in observing the ordinances of God."[16] But then a skeptic named Korihor came along, mocking the Savior's gospel, calling it the "foolish" and "silly traditions of their fathers."[17] Korihor led "away the hearts of many, causing them to lift up their heads in their wickedness."[18] But others he could not deceive, because to them, the gospel of Jesus Christ was much more than a tradition.[19]

Faith is strong when it has deep roots in personal experience, personal commitment to Jesus Christ, independent of what our traditions are or what others may say or do.

Our testimony will be tested and tried. Faith is not faith if never tested. Faith is not strong if never opposed. So don't despair if you have trials of faith or unanswered questions.

We should not expect to understand everything before we act. That is not faith. As Alma taught, "Faith is not to have a perfect knowledge of things."[20] If we wait to act until all of our questions are answered, we severely limit the good we can accomplish, and we limit the power of our faith.

Faith is beautiful because it persists even when blessings don't come as hoped for. We can't see the future, we don't know all the answers, but we can trust Jesus Christ as we keep moving forward and upward because He is our Savior and Redeemer.

Faith endures the trials and the uncertainties of life because it is firmly rooted in Christ and His doctrine. Jesus Christ, and our Father in Heaven who sent Him, together constitute the one undeviating, perfectly reliable object of our trust.[21]

A testimony is not something that you build once and it stands forever. It's more like a tree that you nourish constantly. Planting the word of God in your heart is only the first step. Once your testimony starts to grow, then the real work begins! That's when you "nourish it with great care, that it may get root, that it may grow up, and bring forth fruit." It takes "great diligence" and "patience with the word." But the Lord's promises are sure: "Ye shall reap the rewards of your faith, and your diligence, and patience, and long-suffering, waiting for the tree to bring forth fruit unto you."[22]

My dear brothers and sisters, my dear friends, there's a part of me that misses the old Zwickau chapel and its stained-glass windows. But over the past 75 years, Jesus Christ has led me on a journey through life that is more thrilling than I could ever have imagined. He has comforted me in my afflictions, helped me to recognize my weaknesses, healed my spiritual wounds, and nourished me in my growing faith.

It is my sincere prayer and blessing that we will constantly nourish the roots of our faith in the Savior, in His doctrine, and in His Church. Of this I testify in the sacred name of our Savior, our Redeemer, our Master—in the name of Jesus Christ, amen.

Notes

1. The year 2024 also marks 30 years since my call as a General Authority and 25 years since our family had to move from Germany to the United States as a result of that calling. And almost exactly 20 years ago—on October 2, 2004—I was sustained as a member of the Quorum of the Twelve Apostles and a special witness "of the name of Christ in all the world" (Doctrine and Covenants 107:23).
2. In some ways, my feelings about that building are like what Alma's people felt about the Waters of Mormon—it was a beautiful place to them because "there [they] came to the knowledge of their Redeemer" (Mosiah 18:30).
3. Matthew 24:35; see also Joseph Smith—Matthew 1:35.
4. Isaiah 54:10; see also 3 Nephi 22:10.
5. President Thomas S. Monson taught this same truth with these words: "I believe that among the greatest lessons we are to learn in this short sojourn upon the earth are lessons that help us distinguish between what is important and what is not. I plead with you not to let those most important things pass you by" ("Finding Joy in the Journey," *Ensign* or *Liahona*, Nov. 2008, 85). Similarly, when President Russell M. Nelson recently encouraged us to "think celestial," he said, "Mortality is a master class in learning to choose the things of greatest eternal import" ("Think Celestial!," *Liahona*, Nov. 2023, 118).
6. *Teachings of Presidents of the Church: Joseph Smith* (2007), 264; see also *Teachings of Presidents of the Church: Brigham Young* (1997), 16–18.
7. *Teachings: Joseph Smith*, 49.
8. John 15:4.
9. Matthew 23:23, New Revised Standard Version.
10. Is it interesting to note archaeological similarities between ancient American cultures and Book of Mormon peoples? It can be. Is it helpful to learn from the accounts of scribes and others about the details of how Joseph Smith translated the Book of Mormon? It is for some. But none of this constitutes a lasting testimony that the Book of Mormon is the word of God. For that, you need to find the Savior in the Book of Mormon, to hear His voice speaking to you. Once this happens, it won't matter to you where the ancient city of Zarahemla was actually located or what the Urim and Thummim looked like. Those are branches that can be pruned off your tree if needed, but the tree will remain.
11. See Doctrine and Covenants 84:19–20.
12. See Joy D. Jones, "For Him," *Ensign* or *Liahona*, Nov. 2018, 50–52.
13. See Genesis 3:18.
14. President Nelson has invited all of us "to take charge of [our] own testimony of Jesus Christ and His gospel. Work for it. Nurture it so that it will grow" ("Overcome the World and Find Rest," *Liahona*, Nov. 2022, 97).
15. Colossians 2:7.
16. Alma 30:3.
17. See Alma 30:12–16, 31.
18. Alma 30:18.
19. Interestingly, Korihor's arguments were entirely unpersuasive among the recently converted

Lamanites, the people of Ammon (see Alma 30:19–20), who were following Christ not because of the tradition of their fathers.

By contrast, the Book of Mormon also tells of a generation of young people who separated themselves from the Lord's Church because "they did not believe the tradition of their fathers" (see Mosiah 26:1–4). It's good for families to establish righteous traditions. But it's just as important for families to clearly understand the *why* behind those traditions. Why do we pray every morning and night? Why do we have family scripture study? Why do we hold weekly home evening, family activities and service projects, and so on? If our children understand how these traditions draw us closer to Heavenly Father and Jesus Christ, they'll be more likely to continue them—and improve on them—in their own families.

20. Alma 32:21. Faith is powerful not because of what it *knows* but because of what it *does*.
21. See Hebrews 10:23.
22. Alma 32:37, 41–43.

THE WORDS OF CHRIST AND THE HOLY GHOST WILL LEAD US TO THE TRUTH

ELDER TAKASHI WADA

Of the Seventy

God is our Father in Heaven.[1] We are His spirit children, and we are created after His image.[2] Therefore, each of us, as a child of God, has a divine potential to become like Him.

We lived with Him as spirits before we came to this earth.[3] Heavenly Father, as our spirit parent, loves us, wants the best for us, and prepared a plan for us to receive His greatest blessings, which are immortality and eternal life.[4] According to the plan, we, as spirit children, would be given agency to choose His plan.[5] By coming to the earth, we would leave God's presence, forget our premortal life, receive bodies of flesh and bones, gain our own experience, and develop faith.[6] With our bodies of flesh and bones, as natural men we would succumb to temptation, become unclean and distant from God, and not be able to return to His holy presence. Because of Heavenly Father's infinite love for us, He sent His Firstborn Son, Jesus Christ, to be our Savior. Through His sacrifice, the Atonement, Jesus Christ made it possible for us to be redeemed from our sins and be resurrected and receive eternal life.[7]

I am extremely grateful for these glorious truths—what we call the Father's plan of salvation, His plan of mercy, or His great plan of happiness. Learning these important truths has helped me know my true identity and the great blessings of exaltation and eternal life God has prepared for us. The prophet Nephi taught us the way: "Wherefore, . . . feast upon the words of Christ; for behold, the words of Christ will tell you all things what ye should do."[8] He added, "If ye will enter in by the way, and receive the Holy Ghost, it will show unto you all things what ye should do."[9] Today I would like to share how the words of Christ and the Holy Ghost helped me find these important peace-giving truths in my teenage years.[10]

The Words of Christ Will Tell You All Things What You Should Do

Just like Nephi stated in the opening verse of the book of 1 Nephi, I was also "born of goodly parents."[11] I grew up in Nagano, Japan, in a home where honesty, diligence, and humility were strongly encouraged and conformity to the old customs was strictly followed. My father was a very religious man. I watched him praying in front of the Shinto and Buddhist altars every morning and every night. Even though I had no idea whom he was praying to and what he was praying for, I believed some sort of unseen power or God would be "mighty to save" or help us if we prayed sincerely.[12]

Like other teenagers, I experienced many hardships. I struggled, thinking that life was unfair and had lots of ups and downs. I felt lost, not having a sense of direction in my life. Life seemed so fleeting because it would end when I died. Life without knowing the plan of salvation was confusing.

Not long after I started to learn English in junior high school, all the students in our school received a copy of the New Testament.[13] Though we had barely begun our study of English, our teacher told us we should study English by reading it. I opened it and reviewed its contents. The words in the New Testament were extremely difficult for me. The words in Japanese were equally difficult. However, I was drawn to a list of statements and questions of the soul that had been included just before the biblical text in this Gideon Bible—questions about feeling lonely, lacking confidence, being confused, facing life's trials, and so on. Each item on the list was followed by a reference to verses and pages in the New Testament. I was especially drawn to the statement "When you are weary." The reference led me to open Matthew 11:28–30, in which Jesus said to His disciples:

"Come unto me, all ye that labour and are heavy laden, and I will give you rest.

"Take my yoke upon you, and learn of me; for I am meek and lowly in heart: and ye shall find rest unto your souls.

"For my yoke is easy, and my burden is light."

This was the first time I remember reading the words of Jesus

Christ. Though I did not understand all the words He said, His words comforted me, lifted my soul, and gave me hope. The more I read His words, the more I felt like I should try the virtue of His words.[14] I had never felt like I felt that day. I felt I was loved. I felt that Jesus Christ was someone I knew.

As I continued studying, I felt as though He were speaking directly to me when He said, "Blessed are they which do hunger and thirst after righteousness: for they shall be filled."[15]

His words filled my heart, even though I could not describe my feelings well at that time. Although Jesus Christ lived many centuries ago in a land unfamiliar to me, I thought I could trust His words with all my heart. I hoped someday in the future I might learn more about Jesus Christ.

The Holy Ghost Will Show You All Things What You Should Do

That someday came only a few years later. I met very dedicated, young, full-time missionaries of The Church of Jesus Christ of Latter-day Saints. And I soon met a small group of kind and joyful Latter-day Saints striving to follow Jesus Christ. Despite it taking me a while to fully trust them, I came to see in the restored gospel what I yearned for when I studied the New Testament—the words of Jesus Christ and the hope and peace that come from them.

A particularly sacred experience was when the missionaries taught me to pray. I learned that we should address God by name. When we pray, we should speak from our hearts, express our gratitude, and share our hopes and desires.[16] Once we have said all that we want to say, we end our prayer by saying, "In the name of Jesus Christ, amen." We do this because Jesus commanded us to pray in His name.[17] Praying to Heavenly Father helped me know who He is and my relationship with Him—that I was His beloved spirit son. I learned that because Heavenly Father knows and loves me, He would speak to me personally, uniquely, and in ways I would understand through the Holy Ghost.[18]

There was a time when I really could not recognize the Holy

Ghost. I misunderstood, thinking that all I had to do was follow the steps of prayer and something dramatic would happen. One day, during a lesson with the missionaries, I stepped out of the lesson to take a break. I was still confused about what I should do with my life if the restored gospel of Jesus Christ really was true.

As I was about to return to the room where the missionaries were waiting, I heard the voice of one of the missionaries. I heard my name. Instead of opening the door, I listened to the voice on the other side of the door. I was stunned. They were simply praying to Heavenly Father. The one saying the prayer was pleading to God that He would hear my prayer. Though his Japanese was not fluent, hearing his sincere prayer softened my heart.[19] I wondered why they cared about me so much. Then I realized that their prayer in my behalf was a reflection of Heavenly Father and the Savior's love for me. That love gave me hope, and afterward I did ask God in faith and with real intent. When I did, I felt a joyful and peaceful feeling that I was indeed a child of God and that I had a divine potential and destiny. The plan of salvation sank deep into my heart.[20]

President Russell M. Nelson has said, "The way you think about who you . . . are affects . . . every decision you will ever make."[21] It is so true for me. The decision to follow the Savior Jesus Christ by being baptized and receiving the gift of the Holy Ghost blessed my life more than I ever imagined. As we enter into the baptismal covenant with God, we promise that we are willing to take upon ourselves the name of Jesus Christ, keep the commandments of God, and serve Him for the remainder of our lives.[22] Our Heavenly Father, in turn, promises us that we can always have His Spirit to be with us—the continued guidance from the Holy Ghost.

I invite you to have faith in the message Nephi taught us—that the words of Christ and the Holy Ghost will direct you to "all things what [you] should do."[23] Everything! This is an incredible gift from God.

Brothers and sisters, I am grateful for our Heavenly Father's plan of salvation. Because He loves us, He prepared the way to return to His presence through His Only Begotten Son, Jesus Christ.

Knowing this incredible plan will help us know we are children of God and we can become like Him. I am grateful for this important truth. I bear you my witness that the words of Jesus Christ and the Holy Ghost will lead us to receive eternal life. I know these things are true. In the sacred name of Jesus Christ, amen.

Notes

1. See Acts 17:29; Romans 8:16; Hebrews 12:9; Doctrine and Covenants 76:24.
2. See Genesis 1:26–27; Moses 2:27.
3. See Jeremiah 1:5; Doctrine and Covenants 93:23; Abraham 3:22–23.
4. See Doctrine and Covenants 14:7; Moses 1:39; Abraham 3:24–27.
5. See 2 Nephi 2:27; Moses 7:32.
6. See Abraham 3:25.
7. See 1 Peter 1:19–20; Revelation 13:8; Moses 4:2; Abraham 3:27; *Preach My Gospel: A Guide to Sharing the Gospel of Jesus Christ* (2023), 50; *General Handbook: Serving in The Church of Jesus Christ of Latter-day Saints*, 1.1, Gospel Library.
8. 2 Nephi 32:3.
9. 2 Nephi 32:5.
10. "Learn wisdom in thy youth" (Alma 37:35).
11. 1 Nephi 1:1.
12. Alma 34:18; see also verse 17.
13. Gideon Bible.
14. See Alma 31:5.
15. Matthew 5:6.
16. See "How to Pray," ChurchofJesusChrist.org.
17. See 3 Nephi 18:19–20.
18. See Camille N. Johnson, "The Savior Speaks to Us Personally, Uniquely, and in Ways We Will Understand," *Inspiration* (blog), June 15, 2022, ChurchofJesusChrist.org.
19. See 1 Nephi 2:16; notice how Nephi's heart was softened after crying unto God.
20. See 1 Kings 19:11–12—felt the still small voice within reaching out to my mind and heart; 1 Nephi 2:16—how God softened Nephi's heart as he prayed; Enos 1:3—the joy of the Saints (the gospel) sunk deep into my heart; Moroni 10:4—pray with real intent.
21. Russell M. Nelson, "Choices For Eternity" (worldwide devotional for young adults, May 15, 2022), Gospel Library.
22. See 2 Nephi 31:13–14; Mosiah 18:10, 13; Doctrine and Covenants 20:37.
23. 2 Nephi 32:3; see also verse 5.

"BEHOLD I AM THE LIGHT WHICH YE SHALL HOLD UP"

ELDER RONALD A. RASBAND
Of the Quorum of the Twelve Apostles

To the many testimonies at this conference, I add my apostolic witness that Jesus Christ is the Son of God, our Lord and Savior, the Redeemer of all of our Father's children. By His Atonement, Jesus Christ made it possible for us, if we are worthy, to return to the presence of our Father in Heaven and be with our families for eternity.

The Savior is not absent from our mortal journeys. For the past two days we have heard Him speak through His chosen leaders that we might draw closer to Him.[1] Time and again, with His pure love and mercy, He sustains us as we face the drama of life. Nephi describes: "My God hath been my support; he hath led me though mine afflictions. . . . He hath filled me with his love."[2]

That love is evident when we sustain one another in His work.

We sustain our living prophet at general conference, and the First Presidency, the Quorum of the Twelve Apostles, General Authorities, and Officers of the Church. To sustain means to *hold up* another person, to give them our attention, to be faithful to their trust, to act upon their words.[3] They speak by inspiration of the Lord; they understand the current issues, the moral decline of society, and the adversary's increasing efforts to thwart the Father's plan. In *holding up* our hands, we are committing our support, not just for that moment but in our daily lives.

Sustaining includes *holding up* our stake presidents and bishops, quorum and organization leaders, teachers, and even camp directors in our wards and stakes. Closer to home, we *hold up* our wives and our husbands, children, parents, extended family, and neighbors. When we *hold up* one another we are saying, "I am here for you, not just to *hold up* your arms and hands when they 'hang down'[4] but to be a comfort and strength at your side."

The concept to *hold up* is rooted in scripture. At the Waters of Mormon, the newly baptized Church members committed "to bear one another's burdens, that they may be light; . . . [to] comfort those that stand in need of comfort, and to stand as witnesses of God at all times and in all things, and in all places."[5]

To the Nephites, Jesus said: "*Hold up* your light that it may shine unto the world. *Behold I am the light which ye shall hold up*."[6] We *hold up* the Lord's light when we hold fast to our covenants and when we support our living prophet as he speaks the words of God.

President Russell M. Nelson said, when serving in the Quorum of the Twelve Apostles, "Our sustaining of prophets is a personal commitment that we will do our utmost to uphold their prophetic priorities."[7]

To *hold up* the prophet is a sacred work. We do not sit quietly by but actively defend him, follow his counsel, teach his words, and pray for him.

King Benjamin, in the Book of Mormon, said to the people, "I am like as yourselves, subject to all manner of infirmities in body and mind; yet I have been chosen . . . and was suffered by the hand of the Lord . . . and have been kept and preserved by his matchless power, to serve you with all the might, mind and strength which the Lord hath granted unto me."[8]

Likewise, at age 100, President Nelson has been kept and preserved by the Lord. President Harold B. Lee, at the time a member of the First Presidency, cited the example of Moses standing atop the hill at Rephidim. "The hands of [the President of the Church] may grow weary," he said. "They may tend to droop at times because of his heavy responsibilities; but as we uphold his hands, and as we lead under his direction, by his side, the gates of hell will not prevail against you and against Israel. Your safety and ours depends upon whether or not we follow the ones whom the Lord has placed to preside over his church. He knows whom he wants to preside over this church, and he will make no mistake."[10]

President Nelson draws upon years of serving the Lord. His maturity, wide-ranging experience, wisdom, and consistent receipt of revelation is specifically suited for our day.[11] He has said: "The Church of Jesus Christ of Latter-day Saints is preparing the world for the day when 'the earth shall be full of the knowledge of the Lord' (Isaiah 11:9). . . . This work is empowered by a divine announcement made 200 years ago. It consisted of only seven words: 'This is My Beloved Son. Hear Him!' (see Joseph Smith—History 1:17)."[12]

President Nelson has also said: "There has never been a time in the history of the world when knowledge of our Savior is more personally vital and relevant to *every human soul.* Imagine how quickly the devastating conflicts throughout the world—and those in our individual lives—would be resolved if we all chose to follow Jesus Christ and heed His teachings."[13]

Brothers and sisters, we need to do more lifting and less murmuring, more upholding the word of the Lord, His ways, and His prophet, who has said: "One of our greatest challenges today is distinguishing between the truths of God and the counterfeits of Satan. That is why the Lord warned us to 'pray always, . . . that [we] may conquer Satan, and . . . *escape the hands of the servants of Satan* that do uphold [the adversary's] work' [Doctrine and Covenants 10:5; emphasis added]."[14]

Last April, Sister Rasband and I had the honor of joining our beloved prophet and Sister Nelson for the rededication of the Manti Utah Temple.

President Nelson surprised everyone when he entered the room. Only a very few of us knew he was coming. In his presence, I immediately felt the light and prophetic mantle he carries. The look of joy on the faces of the people personally seeing the prophet will stay with me forever.

In the prayer of rededication, President Nelson petitioned the Lord that His holy house would essentially *hold up* all who entered the temple, "that they may receive sacred blessings and remain worthy and faithful to their covenants . . . that this may be a house of peace, a house of comfort, and a house of personal revelation for all who enter these doors worthily."[15]

We all need to be lifted up by the Lord with peace, with comfort, and most of all with personal revelation to counter the fear, darkness, and contention encompassing the world.[16]

Before the service, we stood outside in the sun with President and Sister Nelson to view the beautiful setting. President Nelson's ancestral ties to the area run deep. His eight great-grandparents settled in the valleys surrounding the temple, as did some of mine. My great-grandfather Andrew Anderson served on the construction crew of early pioneers who labored 11 years to complete the Manti Temple, the third in the Rocky Mountains.[17]

As we stood with President Nelson, we had the opportunity to *hold up* and support the prophet of God in celebration of the rededication of the Lord's holy house. It was a day I will never forget.

"We build temples to honor the Lord," President Nelson said that sacred day. "They are built for worship and not for show. We make sacred covenants of eternal significance inside these sacred walls."[18] We are gathering Israel.

President Nelson and the prophets before him have cradled the holy temples in their arms. Today, around the world, we have 350 sacred houses of the Lord that are operating, announced, or under construction. As prophet, since 2018, President Nelson has announced 168 temples.[19]

"In our time," he has said, "a whole, complete, and perfect union of all dispensations, keys, and powers are to be welded together (see Doctrine and Covenants 128:18). For these sacred purposes, holy temples now dot the earth. I emphasize again that construction of these temples may not change your life, but your service in the temple surely will."[20]

"The Savior and His doctrine are the very heart of the temple," the President says. "Everything taught in the temple, through instruction and through the Spirit, increases our understanding of Jesus Christ. His essential ordinances bind us to Him through sacred priesthood covenants. Then, as we keep our covenants, He endows us with *His* healing, strengthening power."[21]

"All who worship in the temple," President Nelson has said, "will have the power of God and angels having 'charge over them'

[Doctrine and Covenants 109:22]. How much does it increase your confidence to know that, as an endowed woman or man [or temple-attending youth] armed with the power of God, you do not have to face life alone? What courage does it give you to know that angels really will help you?"[22]

Angels reaching out to *hold us up* is described in the scriptures when Jesus Christ knelt humbly in the Garden of Gethsemane. By His suffering He provided an infinite Atonement. "There," President Nelson states, "the greatest single act of love of all recorded history took place. . . . There at Gethsemane, the Lord 'suffered the pain of all men, that all . . . might repent and come unto him' [Doctrine and Covenants 18:11]."[23]

"Remove this cup from me," Jesus Christ asked, "nevertheless not my will, but thine, be done.

"And there appeared an angel unto him from heaven, strengthening him."[24]

We have angels round about us today. President Nelson has said, "[In the temple,] you will learn how to part the veil between heaven and earth, how to ask for God's angels to attend you."[25]

Angels bring light. God's light. To His Nephite Apostles, Jesus said, "Behold I am the light which ye shall hold up."[26] As we sustain our prophet, we testify he is called of our Savior, who is "the light . . . of the world."[27]

Dear President Nelson, on behalf of the members and friends of the Lord's Church throughout the world, we feel blessed to *hold up* your teachings, to *hold up* your example of Christlike living, and to *hold up* your fervent testimony of our Lord and Savior, the Redeemer of us all.

I bear my apostolic witness that Jesus Christ is "the light . . . of the world."[28] May we all, as His disciples, "hold up" His light. In the name of Jesus Christ, amen.

Notes

1. See Doctrine and Covenants 1:38.
2. 2 Nephi 4:20–21.
3. See Ronald A. Rasband, "Words Matter," *Liahona*, May 2024, 70–76.
4. Doctrine and Covenants 81:5.

5. Mosiah 18:8–9.

6. 3 Nephi 18:24; emphasis added.

7. Russell M. Nelson, "Sustaining the Prophets," *Ensign* or *Liahona*, Nov. 2014, 75.

8. Mosiah 2:11.

9. See Doctrine and Covenants 21:6; 81:5.

10. Harold B. Lee, in Conference Report, Oct. 1970, 153.

11. In "The Restoration of the Fulness of the Gospel of Jesus Christ: A Bicentennial Proclamation to the World," it states: "We gladly declare that the promised Restoration goes forward through continuing revelation. The earth will never again be the same, as God will 'gather together in one all things in Christ' (Ephesians 1:10)."

12. Russell M. Nelson, "The Future of the Church: Preparing the World for the Savior's Second Coming," *Ensign*, Apr. 2020, 12–13; or *Liahona*, Apr. 2020, 6–7.

13. Russell M. Nelson, "Pure Truth, Pure Doctrine, and Pure Revelation," *Liahona*, Nov. 2021, 6.

14. Russell M. Nelson, "The Power of Spiritual Momentum," *Liahona*, May 2022, 99.

15. "Dedicatory Prayer, Manti Utah Temple, 21 April 2024," ChurchofJesusChrist.org.

16. In the Book of Mormon, the prophet Mormon tried to comfort his son Moroni in a letter when Moroni was alone and hunted by enemies. He wrote, "May Christ lift thee up, and may his sufferings and death . . . rest in your mind forever" (Moroni 9:25).

17. Before the dedication of the Manti Utah Temple in 1888, two other temples in Utah had already been dedicated: the St. George Utah Temple in 1877 and the Logan Utah Temple in 1884. The first temple of the Restoration was built in Kirtland, Ohio, and dedicated in 1836. Great spiritual manifestations accompanied the services, and priesthood keys were restored by Moses, Elias, and Elijah so that temple work and the gathering of Israel could begin in earnest.

    Joseph Smith recorded, "It was a Pentecost and an endowment indeed, long to be remembered, for the sound shall go forth from this place into all the world, and the occurrences of this day shall be handed down upon the pages of sacred history to all generations, as the day of Pentecost, so shall this day be numbered and celebrated as a year of Jubilee and time of rejoicing to the Saints of the Most High God" (Joseph Smith, Journal, 1835–1836, pp. 189–90, josephsmithpapers.org; spelling, capitalization, and punctuation modernized). The Nauvoo Temple was dedicated officially in May 1846, after the majority of the Saints had abandoned their homes and community. More than 6,000 Saints made temple covenants before fleeing to the West. (See Church History Topics, "Nauvoo Temple," Gospel Library.)

18. Russell M. Nelson, in "President Nelson Rededicates Manti Utah Temple," Apr. 21, 2024, newsroom.ChurchofJesusChrist.org.

19. See Scott Taylor, "A By-the-Numbers Look at the 168 Temples Announced by President Nelson," *Church News*, Apr. 14, 2024, thechurchnews.com.

20. Russell M. Nelson, "The Future of the Church," 8–9.

21. Russell M. Nelson, "The Temple and Your Spiritual Foundation," *Liahona*, Nov. 2021, 93–94.

22. Russell M. Nelson, "Rejoice in the Gift of Priesthood Keys," *Liahona*, May 2024, 121.

23. Russell M. Nelson, "The Atonement," *Ensign*, Nov. 1996, 35.

24. Luke 22:42–43.

25. Russell M. Nelson, "The Temple and Your Spiritual Foundation," 96.

26. 3 Nephi 18:24.

27. 3 Nephi 11:11.

28. 3 Nephi 11:11.

SACRED SCRIPTURES—
THE FOUNDATIONS OF FAITH

ELDER QUENTIN L. COOK
Of the Quorum of the Twelve Apostles

My wife, Mary, and I recently saw a T-shirt with the picture of a book and a message on the front which read, "Books: The Original Handheld Device."

I thought about this interesting message and how significant handheld devices of all kinds have become. Upon further contemplation, I realized that any device or even one equipped with artificial intelligence will never be as important or significant as the spiritual guidance that comes from divine revelation.

Whether handheld or digital, the Holy Bible and the Book of Mormon: Another Testament of Jesus Christ provide spiritual guidance and teaching from Jesus Christ, the Savior of the world. We treasure these books for their profound role in documenting God's direction to ancient prophets and people and the guidance they provide for our own personal lives.

Combined with the teachings of living prophets, these sacred scriptures provide doctrinal direction for us in today's world. These scriptures are most powerful when they give instruction, correction,[1] comfort, and consolation to individuals and families who seek guidance from the Lord.

The scriptures, combined with spiritual inspiration from the Holy Spirit, continue to be the primary source that facilitates the conversion of those who have broken hearts and contrite spirits[2] and desire to follow Jesus Christ. The scriptures help build a foundation that can withstand the adversary's constant efforts to undermine faith.

New converts have blessed and been the lifeblood of the Church throughout its history. One example is particularly precious to me. When I was a young bishop, two marvelous sister missionaries[3] were teaching the William Edward Mussman family. The father, a very capable lawyer, was general counsel of a major corporation. His devoted wife, Janet, was helping the family strive to live a more Christlike life.

Their exceptional son and daughter,[4] both in their early 20s, were also being taught. All four had received the lessons and were attending church. The sister missionaries had emphasized reading the Book of Mormon and praying for a testimony of that sacred scripture. Remarkably, the family prayerfully read the entire Book of Mormon in a short time.

The stake missionaries, both of whom were prior ward Relief Society presidents, accompanied them to sacrament meetings.[5]

As the family was nearing baptism, they received a barrage of literature critical of the Church. This was before the internet, but the material filled a large cardboard box.

The sister missionaries invited me as a recently called 34-year-old bishop to help answer the questions being raised. When we gathered in their living room, the large box of pamphlets critical of the Church was in the middle of the room. I had prayerfully approached this assignment. During the opening prayer, the Spirit whispered to me, "He already knows it is true." This was important. The sisters believed that the rest of the family already had a testimony. They were unsure about the father.

I immediately informed him that the Spirit had prompted me that he already had a testimony. "Was that true?" He looked at me intently and said that the Spirit had confirmed the truth of the Book of Mormon and the Church to him.

I then asked whether it would be necessary to review the pamphlets, if they already had a spiritual confirmation.

The father replied that it would not be necessary. The rest of the family concurred with his answer.

He said he did have a significant question: One reason they had received so much literature opposing the Church was that they were members of another faith. In addition, he had made a large pledge to help build a new chapel for that faith. He informed me that the sister missionaries had taught him about the importance of tithing, which he gratefully accepted, but he wondered if it would be wrong to also honor the pledge he had previously made. I assured him that payment of the pledge would be both honorable and appropriate.

The entire family was baptized. One year later they were sealed as a family in the Oakland California Temple. I was privileged to be present. The son completed law school, passed the California Bar Exam, and immediately served a faithful mission in Japan. I have watched over the years as the succeeding generations have remained faithful to the gospel. I was privileged to officiate at the sealing of one of the granddaughters.

The conversions that are occurring in our day are equally remarkable. Last June, Coach Andy Reid, head football coach of the Kansas City Chiefs, and I, along with others[6] representing our faith and other faiths, spoke in a multifaith event at the Riverside Church in New York City. Coach Reid emphasized second chances and responding to invitations and opportunities,[7] which is what the gospel of Jesus Christ is all about. The next morning, with our wives, Tammy Reid and Mary, we attended the sacrament meeting at the Manhattan Second Ward. It was a spiritual service. There were many new converts in the congregation. Five recently baptized members, four men and one young man, were among the Aaronic Priesthood members passing the sacrament. I am happy to report that a similar influx of new members is happening throughout the Church.[8]

We are grateful for the noticeable increase in those who respond to sacred invitations, change their lives, and accept the opportunity to follow Jesus Christ. They enter the covenant path through faith, repentance, baptism, and confirmation as taught in the Holy Bible and the Book of Mormon.

We cannot underestimate the significance of sacred scriptures both in conversions and in remaining faithful in the gospel. The ancient prophets described in the Book of Mormon knew about the mission of Jesus Christ and taught His gospel. The Book of Mormon helps us draw closer to God as we learn, understand, and apply its teachings.[9] The Prophet Joseph Smith taught, "A man [or woman] would get nearer to God by abiding by [the book's] precepts, than by any other book."[10]

To know that the Book of Mormon is the word of God, we need to read, ponder, and pray about it and then act according to its precepts.[11] The prophet Moroni promised that God will reveal the truth of the book to us as we pray with a sincere heart, with real intent, and with faith in Christ.[12] Studying the Book of Mormon is essential for enduring conversion.

As we contemplate the relationship between the Bible and the Book of Mormon as handheld devices, one might ask a question. How useful and complementary do you think two books would be if the Lord declared they would be joined together and "become one in thine hand"? That is what the Lord declared concerning the "stick of Judah," the Bible, and the "stick of Joseph," the Book of Mormon.[13]

In many significant respects, the Book of Mormon provides fundamental doctrine that enhances and builds upon the Bible. The doctrine of the Atonement of Jesus Christ is a profound example.

The Bible provides an accurate account of the mortal ministry of Jesus Christ, including His death and Resurrection. The Book of Mormon is more explicit about the Atonement of Jesus Christ,[14] something prophets explained in detail prior to His death.

The heading to Alma chapter 42 reflects the doctrinal significance of the Atonement of Jesus Christ.

It reads: "Mortality is a probationary time to enable man to repent and serve God—The Fall brought temporal and spiritual death upon all mankind—Redemption comes through repentance—God Himself atones for the sins of the world—Mercy is for those who repent—All others are subject to God's justice—Mercy comes because of the Atonement—Only the truly penitent are saved."

President Russell M. Nelson has said, "I promise that as you prayerfully study the Book of Mormon *every day*, you will make better decisions—*every day*." He also promises that if "you daily immerse yourself in the Book of Mormon, you can be immunized against the evils of the day."[15]

As I mentioned, I was impressed with the concept of the original handheld device—a book. However, I recognize the incredible significance of the internet in the world today. One modern handheld device can provide the information that historically has filled a major library. We are grateful to live in such a time as this. I am particularly grateful that it allows sacred books and Church materials to be available digitally. The internet is a powerful tool for studying the gospel.[16] Today, many people share scriptures with friends using technology. The Book of Mormon app, for example, is a wonderful way to introduce friends to the Book of Mormon and can easily be shared in normal and natural ways wherever you may be.

While the internet provides many blessings, unfortunately, like the written pamphlets critical of the Church I described earlier, it has also been used to create doubt and undermine faith in precious gospel principles. It can be part of the "evils of the day" that President Nelson mentioned.

The adversary and those who assist him, knowingly or unwittingly, have created on the internet the equivalent of the box full of written material critical of the Church I described earlier, intended to draw you away from God's truth.

The issues raised to create doubt over the years have been remarkably similar. This is especially true when you compare our day with the 1960s, when I was in my 20s.[17]

The scriptures teach us to use judgment and be wise in all things. The internet can be used in a positive way or a destructive way.

Both long-term members and those newly studying the gospel need to be intentional about what they view. Do not entertain immoral, dishonest, or unrighteous material. If you do, algorithms can lead you down a path that destroys faith and impairs your eternal progression. You can be acted upon positively or negatively. Seek righteousness and avoid dark internet rabbit holes and doomscrolling.[18] Fill your life with positive, righteous ideas; be joyful; have fun but avoid foolishness. There is a difference. The thirteenth article of faith is a marvelous guide. Above all, immerse yourself regularly in the Book of Mormon, which will draw the Spirit into your life and help you discern truth from error.

My counsel for those who have in any way deviated from the covenant path is to return to the sacred scriptures, prophetic guidance, religious observance in the home, and the music of faith. Every soul is precious to the Lord.[19] We need you! The Lord needs you, and you need Him! You will always be welcome. During my many years of Church service, I have cherished the wonderful people who returned to the covenant path and then served and blessed everyone they loved or with whom they came in contact.

The sacred scriptures and living prophets are a major way a loving Heavenly Father makes His plan of happiness available to all His children.

I bear my sure witness of the divinity of Jesus Christ and the reality of His Atonement, in the name of Jesus Christ, amen.

Notes

1. See 2 Timothy 3:16.
2. See *Preach My Gospel: A Guide to Sharing the Gospel of Jesus Christ* (2023), 28; see also 2 Nephi 2:7; 3 Nephi 12:19; Doctrine and Covenants 20:37; Ezra Taft Benson, "A Mighty Change of Heart," *Ensign*, Oct. 1989, 2–5.
3. Sisters Beverly Bridge and Cheryl Morgan were the sister missionaries.
4. The son, William E. Mussman III, had graduated from Stanford and was attending law school at the University of California, in San Francisco. His sister, Ann C. Mussman, was attending Stanford University.
5. Sisters Eleanor Mehr and Louise Johnson were the stake missionaries.
6. The New York Latter-day Saint Professional Association (NYLDSPA) honored Reverend A. R. Bernard and Coach Andrew "Andy" W. Reid at the historic interdenominational Riverside Church in Manhattan. Church leaders from our faith and many other faiths were also present, including prior honoree Rabbi Joseph Potasnik.
7. See Tad Walch, "How Andy Reid's Beliefs in Jesus Christ and a Second Chance for Michael Vick Guide the Kansas City Chiefs," *Deseret News*, July 3, 2024, deseret.com.
8. Over 198,000 new converts have been baptized between January 1, 2024, through August 30, 2024 (information provided by the Missionary Department).
9. *Preach My Gospel* chapter 5 describes why the Book of Mormon is the keystone of our religion.
10. Introduction to the Book of Mormon.
11. The Prophet Joseph Smith testified that a man would get nearer to God by abiding by the precepts taught in the Book of Mormon than by any other book (see the introduction to the Book of Mormon).
12. See Moroni 10:4.
13. See Ezekiel 37:15–17; see also 2 Nephi 3:12.
14. The word *Atonement*, referring to the Atonement of Jesus Christ, is mentioned only once in the New Testament (see Romans 5:11). In the Book of Mormon, the word *Atonement* is referenced 24 times. 2 Nephi 2:10 describes "the happiness" which is affixed through the Atonement (see also index to the Book of Mormon, "Jesus Christ, Atonement through").
15. Russell M. Nelson, "The Book of Mormon: What Would Your Life Be Like without It?," *Ensign* or *Liahona*, Nov. 2017, 62–63.
16. Just think how blessed we are every week as we study from *Come, Follow Me* online.
17. Some of the issues are simply untrue. Some take historical facts out of context. Some are advocating for social issues that are inconsistent with both the Bible and the Book of Mormon. Some are on issues that the Lord has not yet provided revelation.
18. Doomscrolling is the act of habitually and obsessively searching for negative or depressing news on social media or news feeds (see *Merriam-Webster.com Dictionary*, "doomscroll").
19. The Church has experienced significant growth and increased attendance in recent years. The percent leaving the Church is less than in the past, but we need every member.

SONS AND DAUGHTERS OF GOD

ELDER RUBÉN V. ALLIAUD
Of the Seventy

Today I would like to address one of the most joyful, glorious, and powerful gospel truths that God has revealed. At the same time, it is ironically one for which we have been criticized. An experience I had some years ago profoundly deepened my appreciation for this gospel truth.

As a representative of the Church, I was once invited to a religious conference where it was announced that from that moment on they would recognize as valid all baptisms performed by almost all other Christian churches, as long as the ordinance was done with water and in the name of the Father and of the Son and of the Holy Ghost. Then it was explained that this policy did not apply to baptisms performed by The Church of Jesus Christ of Latter-day Saints.

After the conference I was able to delve deeper into the reasons for that exception with the leader in charge of the announcement. We had a wonderful and insightful conversation.

In short, he explained to me that that exception had primarily to do with our particular beliefs about the Godhead, which other Christian denominations often refer to as the Trinity. I expressed my appreciation for him taking the time to explain to me his beliefs and the policy of his church. At the end of our conversation, we hugged and then said goodbye.

As I later contemplated our discussion, what this leader said about Latter-day Saints not understanding what he called the "mystery of the Trinity" stayed in my mind. What was he referring to? Well, it had to do with our understanding of the nature of God. We believe that God the Father "is an exalted man" with a glorified "body of flesh and bones as tangible as man's; [and] the Son also."[1] Thus, every time we talk about the nature of God, in some way, somehow, we are also talking about our own nature.[2]

And this is true not only because we all were made "in [His] image, after [His] likeness,"[3] but also because, as the Psalmist recorded,

God said, "Ye are gods; and all of you are children of the most High."[4] This is for us a precious doctrine now recovered with the advent of the Restoration. In summary, it is nothing more or less than what our missionaries teach as the first lesson, first paragraph, first line: "God is our Heavenly Father, and we are His children."[5]

Now, you might say, "But many people believe we are children of God." Yes, that is true, but their understanding may be a little different from the implication of its deeper meaning that we affirm. For Latter-day Saints, this teaching is not metaphorical. Rather, we truly believe that we are all literally the children of God. He is "the Father of [our] spirits,"[6] and because of that, we have the potential to become like Him, which seems to be inconceivable to some.

It has now been over 200 years since the First Vision opened the doors to the Restoration. At the time, young Joseph Smith sought guidance from heaven to know what church to join. Through the revelation he received that day,[7] and in later revelations given to him,[8] the Prophet Joseph obtained knowledge about the nature of God and our relationship to Him as His children.

Because of that, we learn more clearly that our Heavenly Father has taught this precious doctrine from the very beginning. Allow me to cite at least two accounts from the scriptures to illustrate this.

You might remember God's instructions to Moses as recorded in the Pearl of Great Price.

We read that "God spake unto Moses, saying: Behold, I am the Lord God Almighty, and Endless is my name." In other words, Moses, *I want you to know who I am*. Then He added, "And, behold, *thou art my son*." Later he said, "And I have a work for thee, *Moses, my son*; and thou art in the similitude of mine Only Begotten." And then finally, He ended with, "And now, behold, this one thing I show unto thee, *Moses, my son*."[9]

It appears that God was determined to teach Moses at least one lesson: "You are my child," which He repeated at least three times. He could not even mention the name of Moses without immediately adding that he was His son.

However, after Moses was left alone, he felt weak because he was no longer in the presence of God. That is when Satan came to tempt him. Can you see a pattern here? The first thing he said was, "Moses, *son of man*, worship me."[10]

In this context, Satan's request to worship him may have been only a distraction. A significant temptation for Moses in that moment of weakness was to become confused and believe that he was only a "son of man," rather than a child of God.

"And it came to pass that Moses looked upon Satan and said: Who art thou? For behold, *I am a son of God*, in the similitude of his Only Begotten."[11] Fortunately, Moses was not confused and did not allow himself to become distracted. He had learned the lesson of who he really was.

The next account is found in Matthew 4. Scholars have entitled this "the three temptations of Jesus," as if the Lord was tempted only three times, which of course is not the case.

Hundreds of gallons of ink have been used to explain the meaning and content of these temptations. As we know, the chapter begins by explaining that Jesus had gone into the desert, "and when he had fasted forty days and forty nights, he was afterward an hungred."

Satan's first temptation apparently had only to do with satisfying the Lord's physical needs. "Command that these stones be made bread," he challenged the Savior.

A second enticement may have had to do with tempting God: "Cast thyself down: for it is written, He shall give his angels charge concerning thee."

Finally, Satan's third temptation referred to the aspirations and glory of the world. After Jesus had been shown "all the kingdoms of the world, . . . [Satan] saith unto him, All these things will I give thee, if thou wilt fall down and worship me."[12]

In truth, Satan's ultimate temptation may have had less to do with those three specific provocations and more to do with tempting Jesus Christ *to question His divine nature*. At least twice, the enticement was preceded by the challenging accusation from Satan: "If thou be the Son of God"[13]—if you really believe it, then do this or that.

Please notice what had happened immediately before Jesus went into the desert to fast and pray: we find the account of Christ's baptism. And when He had come out of the water, there came "a voice from heaven, saying, *This is my beloved Son*, in whom I am well pleased."[14]

Do we see the connection? Can we recognize a pattern here?

It is no wonder that every time we are taught about our divine nature and destiny, the adversary of all righteousness tempts us to call them into question.

How different our decisions would be if we really knew who we really are.

We live in a challenging world, a world of increasing commotion,[15] where honorable people strive to at least emphasize our human dignity, while we belong to a church and embrace a gospel that lift our vision and invite us into the divine.

Jesus's commandment to be "perfect, even as [our] Father which is in heaven is perfect"[16] is a clear reflection of His high expectations and our eternal possibilities. Now, none of this will happen overnight. In the words of President Jeffrey R. Holland, it will happen "eventually."[17] But the promise is that if we "come unto Christ," we will "be perfected in him."[18] That requires a lot of work—not just any work, but a divine work. His work!

Now, the good news is that it is precisely our Father in Heaven who has said, "For behold, this is *my work* and my glory—to bring to pass the immortality and eternal life of man."[19]

President Russell M. Nelson's invitation to "think celestial"[20] implies a wonderful reminder of our divine nature, origin, and potential destination. We can obtain the celestial only through Jesus Christ's atoning sacrifice.

Perhaps that is why Satan enticed Jesus with the very same temptation from the beginning to the end of His earthly ministry. Matthew recorded that while Jesus hung on the cross, those "that passed by reviled him, . . . saying, . . . *If thou be the Son of God*, come down from the cross."[21] Glory be to God that He did not hearken but instead provided the way for us to receive all celestial blessings.

Let us always remember, there was a great price paid for our happiness.

I testify as with the Apostle Paul that "the Spirit itself beareth witness with our spirit, that we are children of God: and if children, then heirs; heirs of God, and joint-heirs with Christ; if so be that we suffer with him, that we may be also glorified together."[22] In the name of Jesus Christ, amen.

Notes

1. *Teachings of Presidents of the Church: Joseph Smith* (2007), 40, 41; see also Doctrine and Covenants 130:22.
2. See 2 Peter 1:4; "The Family: A Proclamation to the World," Gospel Library.
3. Genesis 1:26.
4. Psalm 82:6; see also John 10:34–35.
5. *Preach My Gospel: A Guide to Sharing the Gospel* (2023), 31.
6. Hebrews 12:9.
7. See Joseph Smith—History 1:16–17.
8. See Doctrine and Covenants 130:3, 22.
9. Moses 1:3, 4, 6, 7; emphasis added.
10. Moses 1:12; emphasis added.
11. Moses 1:13; emphasis added.
12. See Matthew 4:1–9.
13. Matthew 4:3, 6.
14. Matthew 3:17; emphasis added.
15. See Doctrine and Covenants 45:26.
16. Matthew 5:48; see also Joseph Smith Translation, Matthew 5:50 (in Matthew 5:48, footnote *a*).
17. Jeffrey R. Holland, "Be Ye Therefore Perfect—Eventually," *Ensign* or *Liahona*, Nov. 2017, 40–42.
18. Moroni 10:32.
19. Moses 1:39; emphasis added.
20. Russell M. Nelson, "Think Celestial!," *Liahona*, Nov. 2023, 117–19.
21. Matthew 27:39–40; emphasis added.
22. Romans 8:16–17.

FOCUS ON JESUS CHRIST AND HIS GOSPEL

ELDER I. RAYMOND EGBO

Of the Seventy

In 1996 the Nigerian men's football team won gold at the Olympic Games held in Atlanta in the United States. As the final ended, jubilant crowds poured onto the streets of every city and town in Nigeria; this country of 200 million people was instantly transformed into a massive celebration at two o'clock in the morning! There was infectious joy, happiness, and excitement as people ate, sang, and danced. In that moment, Nigeria was united and every Nigerian was content being Nigerian.

Before the Olympics, this team faced numerous challenges. As the tournament began, their financial support ended. The team competed without proper kits, training venues, food, or laundry services.

At one point, they were minutes away from being eliminated from competition, but the Nigerian team triumphed against all odds. This pivotal moment changed how they saw themselves. With newfound confidence, and with individual and team hard work and dogged determination, they unitedly ignored distractions and focused on winning. This focus earned them gold medals, and Nigerians christened them the "Dream Team." The Dream Team at the 1996 Olympics continues to be referenced in Nigerian sports.

Once the football team learned to ignore the many distractions facing them and focused on their goal, they succeeded beyond what they thought possible and experienced great joy. (As did the rest of us in Nigeria!)

In a similar way, when we ignore the distractions of the world and focus on Christ and His gospel, we are guaranteed success beyond what we can fully imagine and can feel great joy. President Russell M. Nelson taught: "When the focus of our lives is on . . . Jesus Christ and His gospel, we can feel joy regardless of what is happening—or not happening—in our lives."[1]

I pray that the Holy Ghost will help each of us to heed President

Nelson's invitation to focus our lives on "Jesus Christ and His gospel" so we can experience joy in Christ "regardless of what is happening—or not happening—in our lives."[2]

Several accounts in the Book of Mormon describe individuals who turned their lives around by focusing on Jesus Christ and His gospel.

Consider Alma the Younger. He rebelled and fought against the Church. His father, Alma, prayed and fasted. An angel appeared and called Alma the Younger to repentance. In that moment, Alma began to suffer "the pains of a damned soul."[3] In his darkest hours, he remembered his father teaching that Christ would come to atone for the sins of the world. As his mind caught hold on this thought, he pled with God for mercy. Joy was the result, a joy he described as exquisite![4] Mercy and joy came to Alma because he and his father focused on the Savior.

For parents with children who have strayed, take heart! Instead of wondering why an angel does not come to help your child repent, know that the Lord has placed a mortal angel in his or her path: the bishop, another Church leader, or a ministering brother or sister. If you keep fasting and praying, if you do not set a timetable or a deadline for God, and if you trust that He is stretching forth His hand to help, then—sooner or later—you find God touching the heart of your child when your child chooses to listen. This is so because Christ is joy—Christ is hope;[5] He is the promise "of good things to come."[6] So trust Jesus Christ with your child, for He is the strength of every parent[7] and every child.

Once he experienced joy in Christ, Alma the Younger lived with that joy. But how did he maintain such joy even through difficulty and trial? He states:

"From that time even until now, I have labored without ceasing, [to] bring souls unto repentance; that I might bring them to taste of the exceeding joy of which I did taste. . . .

" . . . And . . . the Lord doth give me exceedingly great joy in the fruit of my labors. . . .

"And I have been supported under trials and troubles of every kind."[8]

Joy in Christ began for Alma when he exercised faith in Him and cried for mercy. Then Alma exercised his faith in Christ by laboring to help others taste of the same joy. These continuous labors produced great joy in Alma even in trials and troubles of every kind. You see, "the Lord loves effort," and effort focused on Him brings blessings.[9] Even severe trials can be "swallowed up in the joy of Christ."[10]

Another group in the Book of Mormon who made Jesus Christ and His gospel the focus of their lives and found joy are those who founded the city Helam—a place where they could raise their children and enjoy the free exercise of their religion. This righteous people living good lives were enslaved by a marauding group and stripped of the fundamental human right to exercise religion. Sometimes bad things happen to good people:

"The Lord seeth fit to chasten his people; yea, he trieth their patience and their faith.

"Nevertheless—whosoever putteth his trust in him the same shall be lifted up at the last day. Yea, and thus it was with this people."[11]

How did this people endure through their trials and suffering? By focusing on Christ and His gospel. Their troubles did not define them; rather, each of them turned to God, likely defining themselves as a child of God, a child of the covenant, and a disciple of Jesus Christ.[12] As they remembered who they were and called upon God, they received peace, strength, and ultimately joy in Christ:

"Alma and his people did . . . pour out their hearts to [God]; and he did know the thoughts of their hearts.

"And it came to pass that the voice of the Lord came to them in their afflictions, saying: Lift up your heads and be of good comfort, for I know of the covenant which ye have made unto me; and I will covenant with my people and deliver them out of bondage."[13]

In response, the Lord did "ease the burdens . . . upon [their] shoulders. . . . Yea, the Lord did strengthen them that they could bear up their burdens with ease, and they did submit cheerfully and with *patience to all the will of the Lord.*"[14] Note that these Saints let their troubles, suffering, and trials be swallowed up in the joy of Christ! Then in due time, He showed Alma the way for escape, and Alma—a prophet of God—led them to safety.

As we focus on Christ and follow His prophet, we too will be led to Christ and the joy of His gospel. President Nelson has taught: "Joy is powerful, and focusing on joy brings God's power into our lives. As in all things, Jesus Christ is our ultimate exemplar, 'who for the joy that was set before him endured the cross' [Hebrews 12:2]."[15]

My mother recently passed away; it was a shock. I love my mother and did not plan on losing her so young. But through her passing, my family and I have experienced both sorrow and joy. I know because of Him, she is not dead—she lives! And I know because of Christ and the priesthood keys restored through the Prophet Joseph Smith, I will be with her again. The sorrow of losing my mom has been swallowed up in the joy of Christ! I am learning that to "think celestial"[16] and "let God prevail"[17] includes focusing on the joy available in Christ.

He lovingly invites, "Come unto me, all ye that labour and are heavy laden, and I will give you rest."[18] In the name of Jesus Christ, amen.

Notes

1. Russell M. Nelson, "Joy and Spiritual Survival," *Ensign* or *Liahona*, Nov. 2016, 82.
2. Russell M. Nelson, "Joy and Spiritual Survival," 82; see also Russell M. Nelson, "Let God Prevail," *Ensign* or *Liahona*, Nov. 2020, 92–95; "The Power of Spiritual Momentum," *Liahona*, May 2022, 97–100.
3. Alma 36:16.
4. See Alma 36:17–21.
5. See 1 Timothy 1:1.
6. Hebrews 9:11.
7. See Dieter F. Uchtdorf, "Jesus Christ Is the Strength of Parents," *Liahona*, May 2023, 55–59.
8. Alma 36:24–27.
9. Russell M. Nelson, in Joy D. Jones, "An Especially Noble Calling," *Ensign* or *Liahona*, May 2020, 16.
10. Alma 31:38.
11. Mosiah 23:21–22.
12. See Russell M. Nelson, "Choices for Eternity" (worldwide devotional for young adults, May 15, 2022), Gospel Library.
13. Mosiah 24:12–13.
14. Mosiah 24:14–15; emphasis added.
15. Russell M. Nelson, "Joy and Spiritual Survival," 82–83.
16. See Russell M. Nelson, "Think Celestial!," *Liahona*, Nov. 2023, 117–20.
17. See Russell M. Nelson, "Let God Prevail," 92–95.
18. Matthew 11:28; see also verses 29–30.

THE LORD JESUS CHRIST WILL COME AGAIN

PRESIDENT RUSSELL M. NELSON

President of the Church of Jesus Christ of Latter-day Saints

My dear brothers and sisters, I am grateful that the Lord has blessed me to speak with you.

In this conference, the Lord has spoken to us through His servants. I urge you to study their messages. Use them as a litmus test of what is true and what is not during the next six months.

The preservation and renovation of the Salt Lake Temple and other areas on Temple Square have been underway for nearly five years. Present projections indicate that this work will be completed by the end of 2026. We are grateful for all who are working on this massive project.

During the last six months, we have dedicated or rededicated nine temples in five countries.[1] Between now and the end of the year, we will dedicate five more.[2]

Today we are pleased to announce plans to construct 17 more temples. Please listen reverently as I announce the locations.

- Juchitán de Zaragoza, Mexico
- Santa Ana, El Salvador
- Medellín, Colombia
- Santiago, Dominican Republic
- Puerto Montt, Chile
- Dublin, Ireland
- Milan, Italy
- Abuja, Nigeria
- Kampala, Uganda
- Maputo, Mozambique
- Coeur d'Alene, Idaho
- Queen Creek, Arizona
- El Paso, Texas
- Huntsville, Alabama
- Milwaukee, Wisconsin

- Summit, New Jersey
- Price, Utah

My dear brothers and sisters, do you see what is happening right before our eyes? I pray that we will not miss the majesty of this moment! The Lord is indeed hastening His work.[3]

Why are we building temples at such an unprecedented pace? Why? Because the Lord has instructed us to do so. The blessings of the temple help to gather Israel on both sides of the veil. These blessings also help to prepare a people who will help prepare the world for the Second Coming of the Lord!

As the prophet Isaiah prophesied, and as memorialized in Handel's *Messiah*, when Jesus Christ returns, "the glory of the Lord shall be revealed, and all flesh shall see it together."[4]

In that day "the government shall be upon his shoulder: and his name shall be called Wonderful, Counsellor, The mighty God, The everlasting Father, The Prince of Peace."[5]

Jesus Christ will govern from both old Jerusalem[6] and the New Jerusalem "built upon the American continent."[7] From these two centers, He will direct the affairs of His Church.

In that day the Lord will be known as "King of Kings, and Lord of Lords." Those who are with Him will be "called, and chosen, and faithful."[8]

Brothers and sisters, now is the time for you and for me to prepare for the Second Coming of our Lord and Savior, Jesus the Christ.[9] Now is the time for us to make our discipleship our highest priority. In a world filled with dizzying distractions, how can we do this?

Regular worship in the temple will help us. In the house of the Lord, we focus on Jesus Christ. We learn of Him. We make covenants to follow Him. We come to know Him. As we keep our temple covenants, we gain greater access to the Lord's strengthening power. In the temple, we receive protection from the buffetings of the world. We experience the pure love of Jesus Christ and our Heavenly Father in great abundance! We feel peace and spiritual reassurance, in contrast to the turbulence of the world.

Here is my promise to you: Every sincere seeker of Jesus Christ will find Him in the temple. You will feel His mercy. You will find answers to your most vexing questions. You will better comprehend the joy of His gospel.[10]

I have learned that the most crucial question we each must answer is this: To whom or to what will I give my life?

My decision to follow Jesus Christ is the most important decision I have ever made. During medical school, I gained a testimony of the divinity of God the Father and His Son, Jesus Christ. Since then our Savior has been the rock upon which I have built my life.[11] That choice has made all the difference! That decision has made so many other decisions easier. That decision has given me purpose and direction. It has also helped me weather the storms of life. Let me share two examples:

First, when my wife Dantzel unexpectedly passed away, I could not reach any of our children. There I was, alone, devastated, and crying out for help. Gratefully, through His Spirit, the Lord taught me why my dear Dantzel had been taken home. With that understanding, I was comforted. Over time, I was better able to cope with my grief. Later, I married my beloved wife Wendy. She was a central part of my second example.

When Wendy and I were on assignment in a distant land, armed robbers put a gun to my head and pulled the trigger. But the gun did not fire. Throughout that experience, both of our lives were threatened. Yet Wendy and I felt an undeniable peace. It was the peace "which passeth all understanding."[12]

Brothers and sisters, the Lord will comfort you too! He will strengthen you. He will bless you with peace, even amidst chaos.

Please listen to this promise of Jesus Christ to you: "I will be on your right hand and on your left, and my Spirit shall be in your hearts, and mine angels round about you, to bear you up."[13]

There is no limit to the Savior's capacity to help you. His incomprehensible suffering in Gethsemane and on Calvary was for you! His infinite Atonement is for you!

I urge you to devote time each week—for the rest of your life—to increase your understanding of the Atonement of Jesus Christ. My heart aches for those who are mired in sin and don't know how to get out. I weep for those who struggle spiritually or who carry heavy burdens alone because they do not understand what Jesus Christ did for them.

Jesus Christ took upon Himself *your* sins, *your* pains, *your* heartaches, and *your* infirmities.[14] You do not have to bear them alone! He will forgive you as you repent. He will bless you with what you need.[15] He will heal your wounded soul.[16] As you yoke yourself to Him, your burdens will feel lighter.[17] If you will make and keep covenants to follow Jesus Christ, you will find that the painful moments of your life are temporary. Your afflictions will be "swallowed up in the joy of Christ."[18]

It is neither too early nor too late for you to become a devout disciple of Jesus Christ. Then you will experience fully the blessings of His Atonement. You will also be more effective in helping to gather Israel.

My dear brothers and sisters, in a coming day, Jesus Christ will return to the earth as the millennial Messiah. So today I call upon you to rededicate your lives to Jesus Christ. I call upon you to help gather scattered Israel and to prepare the world for the Second Coming of the Lord. I call upon you to talk of Christ, testify of Christ, have faith in Christ, and rejoice in Christ![19]

Come unto Christ and "offer your whole [soul]" to Him.[20] This is the secret to a life of joy!

The best is yet to come, my dear brothers and sisters, because the Savior is coming again! The best is yet to come because the Lord is hastening His work. The best is yet to come as we fully turn our hearts and our lives to Jesus Christ.

I bear my solemn witness that Jesus Christ is the Son of God. I am His disciple. I am honored to be His servant. At His Second Coming, "the glory of the Lord shall be revealed, and all flesh shall see it together." That day will be filled with joy for the righteous!

Through the power of the sacred priesthood keys I hold, I

declare this truth to you and to all the world! In the name of Jesus Christ, amen.

Notes

1. Manti Utah Temple rededication (President Russell M. Nelson, April 21); Urdaneta Philippines Temple (President Dallin H. Oaks, April 28); Puebla Mexico Temple (Elder Gerrit W. Gong, May 19); Taylorsville Utah Temple (Elder Gerrit W. Gong, June 2); Cobán Guatemala Temple (Elder Dale G. Renlund, June 9); Salta Argentina Temple (Elder D. Todd Christofferson, June 16); Layton Utah Temple (Elder David A. Bednar, June 16); Pittsburgh Pennsylvania Temple (Elder Dieter F. Uchtdorf, September 15); Mendoza Argentina Temple (Elder Ronald A. Rasband, September 22).
2. San Pedro Sula Honduras Temple (October 13); Salvador Brazil Temple (October 20); Deseret Peak Utah Temple (November 10); Casper Wyoming Temple (November 24); Tallahassee Florida Temple (December 8).
3. See Doctrine and Covenants 88:73.
4. Isaiah 40:5; see also George Frideric Handel, "And the Glory of the Lord," *The Messiah*, ed. T. Tertius Noble (1912), 16–18.
5. Isaiah 9:6.
6. See Zechariah 14:4–7; Doctrine and Covenants 45:48–66; 133:19–21; see also Micah 4:2: "For the law shall go forth of Zion, and the word of the Lord from Jerusalem."
7. Articles of Faith 1:10; see also Ether 13:3–10; Doctrine and Covenants 84:2–4.
8. Revelation 19:16; Revelation 17:14.
9. See Alma 34:32.
10. You may feel to say, as did Ammon, "Who can glory too much in the Lord? . . . Behold, . . . I cannot say the smallest part which I feel" (Alma 26:16).
11. See Helaman 5:12.
12. Philippians 4:7.
13. Doctrine and Covenants 84:88.
14. See Alma 7:11–12; see also Luke 4:18.
15. See Alma 7:12.
16. See Psalm 147:3; Jacob 2:8.
17. See Mosiah 24:14.
18. Alma 31:38.
19. See 2 Nephi 25:26.
20. Omni 1:26.

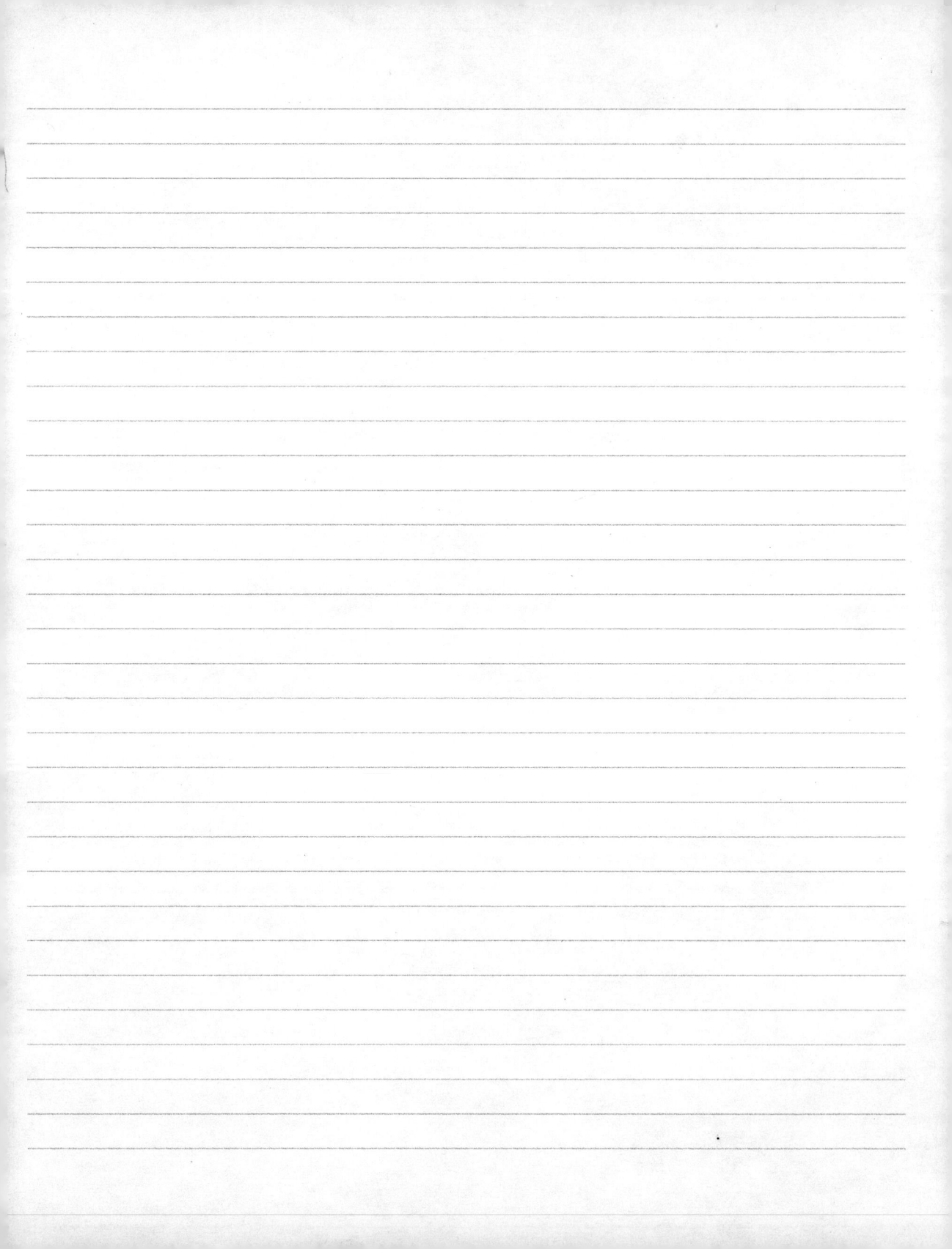